Praise for *Still No Wo*

Finalist for the PEN/Diamonstein-Spielvogel Award for the Art
of the Essay and the Vermont Book Award

"Orner is a highly lauded author whose writing, in both fiction and
nonfiction, is an act of wizardry. In each of these micro-essays,
he reduces the meat of his own life down to the bone, then stirs
in fatty excerpts from hundreds of stories, novels and poems by
writers ranging from Woolf to Rhys, Babel to Kafka."
—Stephanie Elizondo Griest, *The New York Times Book Review*

"So much of the pleasure in this book comes from Orner's impres-
sions of what he's read. There's a piece about Kafka and people
who are 'exceptional readers,' and, finishing this book, I had the
same thought about Peter Orner: it's almost like a parallel life, or
an ongoing dream, the way his reading occupies him, but only an
exceptional writer can make that interior work legible to others."
—Emma Cline, *Literary Hub*

"Like its predecessor collection *Am I Alone Here?*, a 2016 finalist for
the National Book Critics Circle Award in criticism, *Still No Word
from You* is a book of conversations: Orner in dialogue with other
books, Orner in dialogue with himself . . . *Still No Word from You*
looks at its author's life through the lens of reading: memoir as
daybook, as it were. In 107 short essays or chapters (some just a
paragraph), Orner shapeshifts and time travels."
—David Ulin, *Los Angeles Times*

"Yearning for lost time infuses every page of [Peter Orner's] second nonfiction collection . . . It's a meditation on storytelling from

a wide-ranging thinker and reader, mining Orner's past, generations of family history and the many fictional folks swirling around his mind." —L. A. Taggart, *San Francisco Chronicle*

"If there's an ideal autumn book, it's a book about books, writers and reading. *Still No Word from You: Notes in the Margin*, by the always undervalued Peter Orner, swings seamlessly between his Highland Park boyhood (a Cheever tale, writ large) and his reading life, mourning family, and even stumbling on his mother's youthful marginalia." —Christopher Borrelli, *Chicago Tribune*

"A heartfelt memoir in books and marginalia . . . In Peter Orner's *Still No Word from You*, literature and life are inextricably intertwined, each illuminating the other." —Julia M. Klein, *Forward*

"Orner—a legitimate triple-threat: novelist, short story master, and prolific essayist—returns with an addictive collection of more than 100 buoyant essays organized around a single day and a wide range of emotions . . . [A] wise, welcoming, heartfelt book." —*Kirkus Reviews* (starred review)

"Pushcart Prize–winning fiction writer Orner (*Maggie Brown & Others*) brings his lyrical, mosaic style to the story of his own life in this gorgeous and contemplative memoir . . . Evocative and erudite, this meditation on impermanence and its ephemeral joys is a gem." —*Publishers Weekly* (starred review)

"Peter Orner's work clings close to life, to the unadorned, untranscended, dear and haunting Actual." —Marilynne Robinson

"What to call this gloriously strange marvel of a book devoted to other books? Who cares? *Still No Word from You* offers solace to those among us who look out windows, whose minds wander, who are bewildered by time and memory . . . A beautiful testament to the way the books we love are not merely as real as life, they are life." —Maud Casey, author of *City of Incurable Women*

"*Still No Word from You* is a sharp-edged and heartfelt mosaic of the reading life. I know of no other writer working today who so exquisitely and seamlessly brings together storytelling, memoir, essay, and the act of reading as both a visionary and an intimate journey." —Eduardo Halfon, author of *Mourning*

"This is a unique concoction, with essays bleeding into stories, coming out the other side, and creating something new. *Still No Word from You* is a beautiful piece of work that demonstrates the special illumination on life granted by a passion for reading." —Kevin Barry, author of *Night Boat to Tangier*

"Peter Orner is a bard of the corners of life. From there he tells stories that range from broad considerations of the nature of time to intimate portraits of his varied and curious experiences in the world. His insights are sharp and stunning, his stories paced with a poet's rhythm. Orner's voice is mournful and humorous, contemplative but with a taste for the ridiculous. In *Still No Word from You*, life is a strange gift. Read this book to be delighted and entertained, but even more, read it to recover your faith in storytelling itself." —Emily Bernard, author of *Black Is the Body: Stories from My Grandmother's Time, My Mother's Time, and Mine*

Still No Word from You

ALSO BY PETER ORNER

Maggie Brown & Others
Am I Alone Here?: Notes on Living to Read and Reading to Live
Last Car Over the Sagamore Bridge
Love and Shame and Love
The Second Coming of Mavala Shikongo
Esther Stories

As Editor
Lavil: Life, Love and Death in Port-au-Prince
Hope Deferred: Narratives of Zimbabwean Lives
Underground America

Still No Word from You

Notes in the Margin

Peter Orner

Catapult New York

Still No Word from You

First Catapult edition: 2022
First paperback edition: 2023

Hardcover ISBN: 978-1-64622-136-3
Paperback ISBN: 978-1-64622-204-9

Library of Congress Control Number: 2022936129

Cover design by Dana Li
Cover photo © Stocksy / Vero
Book design by Olenka Burgess

Catapult
New York, NY
books.catapult.co

Printed in the United States of America

10 9 8 7 6 5 4 3 2 1

For Katie, Phoebe, and Roscoe

and

Rhoda and Dan Pierce

And the sun that had risen in the morning would fall
to its knees in the evening . . .
—VIEVEE FRANCIS, "Loving Me"

You're a fool. Go on, keep pedaling, it's getting late.
—PRIMO LEVI, *The Periodic Table*

Contents

Morning   1

Mid-Morning   61

Noon   121

3 P.M.   177

Dusk   225

Night   269

Sources   293

Acknowledgments   301

Morning

A house remembers.

—Edna O'Brien

ON THE BLACK-AND-WHITE TV IN THE KITCHEN, MY mother and I watched Richard Nixon's helicopter slowly rise. My mother stood at the sink doing dishes. At one point she stopped scrubbing but left her hands in the dishwater. The kitchen of the house on Hazel Avenue. The house no longer exists. It is less about her expression than that her hands remained in the water but were no longer scrubbing the dishes. Something to do with the stillness, her hands suddenly motionless in the soapy water. Maybe at that moment she wasn't thinking about Nixon at all. Which direction was she looking? Not at the TV. She was staring out at the backyard. The house on Hazel had a back patio with a low brick wall around it. I used to jump off the wall into the grass. The grass in the backyard of the house on Hazel was a deep, luscious green. If you yanked up a strand and pulled, it made a squeaky sound. I'd eat that grass by the mouthful. I don't know which month of 1974 Nixon called it quits. I could check. It's exhausting being able to check anything and everything. Let's say it was spring, late spring, when Nixon resigned, and let it be wrong if it's wrong, and that the grass in the backyard was a deep May green, especially where the shadow of our tall sycamore tree stretched across the lawn. My mother is looking out the window. She wouldn't leave Hazel Avenue, with my brother and me in tow, for almost another decade. But I know I read something in her eyes. As if she'd already taken off. My mother, the sound of her splashing, scrubbing, and then, stillness.

THERE'S A MOMENT IN JAMES SALTER'S "DUSK" WHEN A woman named Mrs. Chandler looks out a store window and sees the past. It's a simple line. "It seemed as if it were years ago." It's a glimpse into the past that makes up any given present, that lurks, always, in the shadow of right now. Mrs. Chandler is only a woman in a small store, looking out the window at the cars going by on the road. She's holding an onion. It's begun to rain. I remember where I was when I first read this scene. I was in the library at San Francisco State, between classes. 2004? 2005? Those years teaching kept me sane. Usually it was the other way around and the sound of my own voice made me cringe. At that time, going on and on, preaching the gospel of fiction kept me tethered, at least slightly, to the existence of other people. Otherwise, I'd have completely retreated, where I'm not exactly sure.

I was already late for my own class. I hadn't finished the story so I walked out with the book. The buzzer sounded. I kept moving. Nobody chased me. I still have it, a stolen orange hardcover, soiled from the grease of my hands.

Mrs. Chandler refuses to drive to the big store out by the highway. She always shops at the little market in town. Though she doesn't buy much anymore. Vera Pini, as always, is perched by the register. Vera tells Mrs. Chandler that she's got some good Brie today. Mrs. Chandler asks, Is it really good? Yes, Vera says, it's very good.

On the plate glass the first drops of rain appear.

Look at that, Vera says, it's started.

And that's when Mrs. Chandler, elegantly dressed Mrs. Chandler, looks out the window into years ago. There's more to the story. Usually there is. But I'm drawn lately to the moments before a story becomes a story. Like opening stage directions. Take *The Cherry Orchard*. It begins: *A room which is still known as the nursery. One of the doors leads to ANYA's room. Half-light, shortly before sunrise. It is May already . . .* The audience still shifting in their seats, tucking away their programs, never hears these lines. They are never spoken out loud. It's a beginning whispered only to a reader.

A woman stands in a store holding an onion. She looks out the window and sees a life that's gone. In the life, her husband and son used to meet her at the train station. I can't remember if she can see the station from where she's standing or not. I'm not sure it matters. All that's in the distance. The narrator tells us, with annoying omniscience, that no one will ever desire Mrs. Chandler again, love her like that again, but—again—that's the story becoming the story, a sad, sadly predictable story, and what I want right now are only these opening notes, the cheese that's very good, the first few drops of rain on the plate glass. Look at that. It's started.

DURING THE SECOND WORLD WAR MY MOTHER'S FATHER was in the civil defense. This was in Fall River, Massachusetts. He carried a gun not much bigger than a cap gun. His responsibility was to make sure his fellow Fall Riverites had their windows properly blacked out. He would walk the streets of his own neighborhood—from Robeson Street to Dudley Street to Highland Avenue—and hunt for light. They wouldn't send him overseas. He was 4-F, back trouble, feet as flat as paper plates. My mother told me he'd painted an old leather football helmet silver and would practice a stern, authoritative face in the bathroom mirror. And if, on his nightly rounds, he spotted a crack of light beyond the blackout curtains, he'd march up to the door, knock on it with four authoritative knuckles, and inform the violators in no uncertain terms that they were aiding and abetting the Luftwaffe by providing an opportunity, a target, a beacon. *Am I being understood?*

Grandpa Freddy was a mild-mannered guy, but give a man a gun, no matter how miniature, and something to enforce and he'll lug the weight of the world across quiet lawns.

Though he'd never gone to college—my Fall River grandparents were seventeen when they eloped and Freddy went right to work—he considered himself a bit of a pointy head. On my shelf, I have his dog-eared Shakespeare's *Collected*

Works, print so small he must have needed a microscope to read it. Still on many of the pages there are notations in the margin, notes to himself. His faded handwriting now unreadable.

My grandfather makes his rounds. I think of him, walking his streets murmuring happily, a Jewish Othello with a bad back: *Put out the light, and then put out the light.*

He really did enjoy those urgent, whispered porch conversations. Not because he so enjoyed berating people or speechifying but because, emerging out of the night to rap on the door of a silent house, he expected the door not only to be answered but for the answerer to listen to him, Fred Kaplan, tell them what was what. *Don't you see? That's what they're after, our light. We've got to hoard the light, not forever, just now.* Him in that goofball silver helmet. A little gun in his pocket. I have the thing here in a drawer. Freddy's paunch, his worn-out loafers. He worked in his father's furniture store. One day the store would be all his. And it was, for a few years. Then, in the '60s, the state of Massachusetts rammed a highway, I-195, through the downtown, like a stake through the heart of Fall River. Entire blocks fell, City Hall, the Hotel Mellen, Kaplan's Furniture. They said it would bring the city business. My grandfather said, A highway will bring business? They'll wave at us on their way to Providence. All that useless destruction would eventually kill him. But during the war he was the third or fourth man on the store's totem pole. He was thirty-six years old. He punched the clock and still called his father sir.

» 4 «

My father's story about how a couple of Irish kids once chased him around the old neighborhood in Rogers Park calling him a kike or a yid or a dirty Jew. One of those, my father couldn't remember exactly. He said it like they were fulfilling an obligation. And he, too, played his role. A little Jew, he ran like hell. When they caught him those two knocked him around, not too bad, enough to make a proper show. They were welcoming my father to the city he'd been born into eight years earlier. Get it? my father would say. *They chased my ass around Rogers Park, not out of it. There's your difference. Others—you know it as well as I do—got chased to hell and gone. You want to know how Chicago works, that's how Chicago—*

I'm running out of stories. Already small to begin with, they're getting even smaller. My father at the corner of Fargo and California, sprinting like mad, those two little Hanrahans gaining on him, kids who have no more idea what a Jew is than they'd have been able to imagine that close to eighty years later someone, me, would be lying in a bed in Vermont next to a sleeping daughter and remembering that they once existed, two little shits who must be dead by now. As dead as the boy they once chased. Sometimes I fall asleep after reading to her and wake and grope around in the dark for a pen and a scrap of paper. Lately, I write down what I've already written. Some stories don't get lost, they get repeated into oblivion.

I get it, Dad. Persecution as initiation.

He always told it like it was something he lived through so he could tell it later. This is how it was to be chased on a late summer day in the mid-1940s. His father was still in the South Pacific. (A Jewish captain in the navy, although you didn't, my grandfather always said, want to be too loud about it.)

Two boys chased my father along the parched brown grass between the sidewalk and the row of parked cars, two little neighbors hell-bent on saying hello.

WHEN I TELL PEOPLE I WAS DISINHERITED THEY ALWAYS look at me like somebody died. Somebody did die, my father died, but I always say I'm over it, the money part anyway. Before he died, I'd always told people that I wouldn't accept a dime from him, not a dime. This was my principled position until I read the part in his will where he wrote my brother and me out of it. I didn't have to look very far. It was in the first paragraph. At that point, I lost my heroic resolve.

I loathe the stuff, I crave the stuff. Isn't this the genius of money?

This past week an Amy Clampitt poem brought back my hypocrite's pain. Not that it takes much. The words *bequest, estate, death tax, a father's love, Don Jr.*—like I say, I'm over it.

In "The Prairie," Clampitt refers to a Jew in a Chekhov story who stuffs six thousand rubles he inherited from *his* father into the stove. Now, there's a man. Here's what I think of your stinking cash. In 1870, six thousand rubles was roughly the equivalent of $4,600, which, adjusted for inflation, would now be $8,317.23. This calculation is according to Dimo_23 on Reddit, who specializes in nineteenth-century currency conversion.

Clampitt writes:

however jaded you may think you are, now
  there's
a scandal for you. Six thousand rubles . . .

In the Chekhov story she's referring to, "The Steppe," the
money burner is named Solomon. His brother Moishe, an
innkeeper, is naturally upset. He shouts, basically, *Look, Solomon, if the money was so goddamn dirty, why in the hell
didn't you just hand it over to me?*

In the way of things, Moishe now has to support his completely destitute brother. He gives him a job at the inn. What
are brothers for?

Clampitt's "The Prairie" is epic, contains multitudes,
runs eleven glorious pages, and casts a wide generational and
geographical net. The poet roams from her own life in Manhattan to her grandfather's meanderings across the country
from Iowa and the Dakotas, out west to California, back east
to Iowa . . .

She mines a mundane coincidence, the fact that her
grandfather and Chekhov were born the same year, 1860; her
grandfather on an Iowa farm, Chekhov in the Russian port
city of Taganrog. And yet, for Clampitt, this takes on broader
significance as she muses on the similarities between the
American prairie and the Russian steppe. This leads her to
Chekhov's Solomon, who mocks us all by stuffing his inheritance in the stove.

Cash. Rare are those who truly believe they can get by
without it. Rarer still are those that actually do. Even Solomon
can't eat his contempt for room and board. Still, Clampitt's
poem is ultimately about the stories we carry across the generations, not the money that does—or doesn't—get passed on.
She recalls her grandfather's brief relocation to the promised

land of the west coast. He lasted only two years before he re-treated to the Midwest. California gave him headaches. We are who we are, not who we strive to be. The man was Iowan to the core.

> What was he good for but what
> he'd been brought up as, a dirt farmer?

Amy Clampitt didn't publish her first book until she was sixty-three. She knew what it was like to bump around, to wander from one job to another. All that time she was working, piling up the details. Our details, our inheritance.

Every day for fifty-four years my father drove to his office on LaSalle Street in Chicago from the suburbs. Let the other fathers, suckers, sit on the train and read the paper. My father was content to wait in traffic on the Kennedy Expressway like some exiled king. In winter, he wore a very tall, furry, Russianish hat. My brother used to say he looked like Leonid Brezhnev's brother.

» **6** «

IN MY MOTHER'S BATTERED COPY OF FERLINGHETTI'S *A Coney Island of the Mind,* she wrote a single word (in light pencil) in the margin of page 29. It's as if she hadn't wanted to deface the book but she couldn't help herself. The poem is about Chagall's mother, how she admonished her son not to let that horse eat that violin but he:

> kept right on
>   painting

To the right of the word *painting* in faint but still, after more than sixty years, readable pencil, in my mother's distinct all-caps handwriting: YES!

Why this particular line caused her to react and talk back to the poem, it's hard to say. She probably thought it was bold that Chagall went ahead and let the horse eat the violin. My mother never much listened to her mother's advice, either.

A Coney Island of the Mind was everywhere in the late 1950s and '60s. My mother's copy is a New Directions paperback published in 1958. The thirty-second printing, according to the copyright page. There's the familiar black-and-white cover of, presumably, Coney Island at night. Ornate, towerlike buildings rising, festooned with lights. Something fantastical about the photograph, suggesting a wondrous, hedonistic carnival. Read this and join the insanity. My mother's copy is well worn, the pages aren't crisp but flimsy, thumbed, as if she read it over and over again.

It was 1959. The year my mother dropped out of Simmons College, married my father, and fled Massachusetts for Chicago. (They'd met at Harvard Summer School, allowing them, and now me, to repeat, *My parents? Oh, they met at Harvard . . .*)

She was twenty-one. He was twenty-three. After an enormous wedding in Fall River—my father's parents chartered a plane to ferry all their friends east from Chicago—the two settled into a little apartment on North State Parkway in Lincoln Park.

Chicago, my god, my mother had never seen anything like it. The movement of the place. Not simply the sheer number of people, bodies, not just the excitement of the frantic day-to-day bustle on the sidewalks, the honking, the shouts, the laughter, the sirens, but how my mother also could feel a pulse beneath all the surface noise, a seething energy that seemed to emanate from the lake itself, brooding out there just a few blocks from their apartment. Lake Michigan, radiant, glistening and yet at the same time, at night, especially at night, menacing and fathomless, came to embody how my mother felt about the city in general, that it was a place where all things were possible. Fall River was spent, a city still feeding, barely, off its last heyday in the 1890s when it produced enough cloth to wrap around the world a thousand times. Chicago didn't hark back to any glorious past. It didn't need to, and besides, it didn't have one. A swamp that smelled of onions? Chicago was the future. And this fit right into how my mother has always—and still does—experience the world, as a place where nothing must ever remain stagnant.

It's likely that she bought her copy of *A Coney Island of the Mind* at the mighty, vast, now vanished citadel of the written word, Kroch's and Brentano's on Michigan Avenue, five floors of books and light and books and books and books. My mother wasn't a beatnik. She'd married an up-and-coming lawyer, and she and my father lived in an apartment building alongside other young professional men and their wives. She was, of course, a Kennedy Democrat, but no, not a beatnik. I'm not sure she would have known what one was exactly, but she'd heard about the Ferlinghetti book and beautiful freaks like Allen Ginsberg and the nutty goings-on in San Francisco and she must have wanted a little of that action. So she bought it, took it home.

>   You and me could really exist
> Wow I says
>   Only the next day
>   she has bad teeth
>   and really hates
>   poetry

I can hear my mother laughing at this, too, in Chicago, in 1959. Bad teeth and really hates poetry! My mother was twenty-six and having the time of her life. Was Ferlinghetti a great poet? Bless him, he never was, but he made my mother laugh.

Wow I says.

Bless all the poets who never become great.

Down the block from my parent's apartment was a bar called the Buttery. It was at the corner of North State and Goethe. In Chicago we say: *Go-thi*. The correct pronunciation can screw itself. The Buttery was inside the Ambassador

West Hotel, and my mother used to go there with her friends from the Alliance Française. My mother, who didn't speak French, was invited into this cultural organization by a high-brow neighbor. You wore a black dress to the Buttery, my mother once told me. A sleeveless black dress, and you talked about France.

Husbands weren't invited to the meetings of the Alliance Française. A heady time for sure. You went to the Buttery to see and be seen. And I think of my mother coming home after one of these nights. My father in the bedroom grinding his teeth in his sleep. My mother's still giddy and so she flops on the couch in the tiny living room (in a couple of years it would become my brother's nursery) and, still wearing high heels, she reads a few more poems out of *A Coney Island of the Mind*. She's always preferred silence to music, my mother, but I can't help giving the moment a soundtrack. Maybe some Coleman Hawkins to accompany these jazzed-up poems. She doesn't think of my father. He doesn't exist. This isn't the point, the point is, no, there is no point. Only my mother, young, so young, holding a book over her head and reading, a little bleary, but at the same time, she's not tired, if anything she's too awake.

FORD MADOX FORD ONCE TRIED TO TELL JEAN RHYS TO add more descriptive passages to her stories. The word he used was *topography*. A reader, he told her, needs to know where he's standing. Your stories are too skeletal, Ford said. They're like you, Jean. Not enough meat on their bones. Ford Madox Ford was the first editor to see something in her work. He knew it was like nobody else's and, like most men at the time, like most men at any time, he felt entitled to mold the work into his own image. He wanted more meat. Yet Rhys liked Ford. For a while, she liked him a lot. He was older (she was in her thirties, he was in his fifties), and common-law married to someone else, but the two (and sometimes the three since, the story goes, the wife was sometimes included) were lovers for a while, in Paris, in the '20s. But sex and conversation and books and good wine were one thing—Jean Rhys's work another.

She went through her stories and hacked every extraneous and not so extraneous description she could find. Fuck topography.

I'm talking here about the early stories, those collected in her first book, *The Left Bank*, published in 1927 with a lengthy preface by Ford. He rattles on, mostly about himself for fifteen pages, before mentioning Rhys and managing to say:

One likes, in short, to be connected with something good, and Miss Rhys' work seems to me
to be so very good, so vivid, so extraordinarily
distinguished by the rendering of passion, and so
true, that I wish to be connected with it.

The Left Bank was followed by four novels, the last of
which, *Good Morning, Midnight,* came out in 1939. And then:
Jean Rhys vanished, not only from the literary scene. She
seemed to vanish off the map itself.

"Vienne," the last story in *The Left Bank,* might be the best of
what I think of as her slash-and-burn period. At twenty-nine
pages "Vienne" reads as if it's weightless. The narrator, Francis, laments that nothing much is left of the days she and her
husband, Pierre, lived high on the hog in Vienna. All that remains are scattered images that loiter in her mind, mostly of
people on the fringe. Vivid images of those she hardly knew,
such as a petite Hungarian dancer, a girl who could jump six
feet and land on a wooden floor without a sound.

> I saw people differently afterwards—because for
> once I'd met sheer loveliness with a flame inside, for
> there was "it"—the spark, the flame in her dancing.

"It" is short-lived. The graceful dancer returns home to
Budapest. Later, Francis hears about her, news Jean Rhys reduces to five words:

> Married to a barber. Rum.

And that's all that's left of the Hungarian dancer. One leap and she's gone for good, from literature, from anywhere. Married to a barber. Rum.

"Vienne" is oddly spare and lush at the same time. Rhys often repeats words, doubles back for emphasis. At first, the husband, Pierre, is an ostentatious success. Money's pouring in from every direction. What does Pierre do to make it? Is he on the up and up? Who cares? Francis doesn't give a damn so long it keeps coming.

> Nice to have lots of money, nice, nice. Goody to
> have a car, a chauffeur, rings, and as many frocks
> as I liked.
> Good to have money, money. All the flowers
> I wanted. All the compliments I wanted. Every-
> thing, everything.
> Oh great god money.

I get woozy. Start to feel like I'm strutting around a casino in Vienna after the First World War, blissful, drunk, tuxedo pockets bulging with cash. But nothing, not a thing, lasts. Again and again, with merciless concision, Rhys destroys her people, her men, yes, but also, especially, her women— typists, secretaries, shop assistants. Soon after they've tasted a little of the good life, Rhys cuts them down.

Francis describes eating in a restaurant where at the very table she's sitting, only a week earlier, another girl, a pretty Russian, newly pregnant, had shot herself.

> With her last money she had a decent meal and
> then bang! Out—

•

Rhys refuses to dwell on the miserable facts that preceded this suicide, facts she knew well enough not to pretend they were unique. The Russian girl flickers as briefly as the Hungarian dancer. We're left to imagine the gory scene at the table without the sort of descriptive lard that Ford was calling for, which makes it a hell of a lot more terrifying.

So long, Vienna. Pierre's shady dealings catch up with him soon enough. The couple flees to Budapest, to Prague. They've got to sell the car, but before they do, they take it out for one last spin. Francis eggs Pierre to drive faster, faster, make this damn thing go! She's hoping to leave it all behind in a crush of metal and glory. But Pierre slows down and Francis has to live with herself another day, like her creator. Jean Rhys never did bang! Out—

She didn't vanish. She didn't disappear. Being broke, drunk, and out of print doesn't mean you don't exist. Biographers have since nosed around. We now know a lot about where she was and what she was doing before she resurfaced. Her first husband went to prison. Her second husband died. Her third, like her first, ended up locked up. We know she was constantly hard up and moving from town to town. Her mental health always tenuous, her drinking nonstop. At one point she went to jail herself for throwing a brick through a neighbor's window. At least she'd had a sound reason. The neighbor's dog had murdered her cat.

In spite of it all, Rhys kept working, trying to work, not working, starting to work . . .

And the story is told on book jackets. How she arose, one leg already in the grave, in 1966 with the typed manuscript of

Wide Sargasso Sea in her gaunt hands, her masterpiece, the great Caribbean novel of her girlhood. It makes for a good myth. The truth is not so clean. She was very much flesh and blood and, like everybody else, consumed by gnawing needs. In 1979, the year she died, Rhys told *The Paris Review*:

> One day in the snow I felt so tired. I thought, "Damn it, I'll sit down. I can't go on. I'm tired of living here in the snow and ice." So I sat down on the ground. But it was so cold I got up.

» 8 «

THERE WERE THOSE PARTIES AT THE BARONS'. LES AND Vanessa Baron's rambling white Colonial on Linden Avenue, the one with the pillars, overlooking the ravines. Les shouting leftist politics. He was a commodities trader. My father said the bigger the house, the bigger the phony. But he loved that house on the ravines. My father craved that house. Everybody did.

Vanessa was tiny and elegant and mostly silent. Late in the night, after more than a few drinks, she'd curl in a chair like a cat while the remaining guests circled, trying to get her attention. If those parties had a center, a beating heart, it was Vanessa Baron, whether she was half asleep or not.

Les gassing on about Jimmy Carter and nuclear proliferation. *Would you look at the defense budget under this full-of-shit peacenik?*

It was said that Les and Vanessa were swingers, though at the time I don't think my brother or I knew what this meant. Also we didn't care. We were down in the ravines with the other kids. Those bowls of dead leaves. That shushing sound the leaves made when we trudged through them. Years of leaves piled on top of one another, and at the bottom, a kind of leaf sludge. It reeked of sewage but at the same time was somehow pure, elemental. And I remember the feeling of being encased, the trees shutting out what little light was left (those parties always started in the late afternoon), and even though all the other kids were shouting across the ravine I could sink down into the leaves and putrid stench and be alone.

Our parents, all the parents, were up and over the lip of the lawn, drinking. Black waiters in gleaming white shirts and bow ties circulated, trays hoisted over their heads.

I guess I credit us, the kids, for understanding something that should have been obvious to our parents—that the suburbs, or to be more specific, our suburb, on the northern shore of Lake Michigan, wasn't simply a parasitical off-shoot of the great city where our fathers worked. No, we understood that we'd been born into an independent landscape with its own history, stolen as it was from slaughtered Potawatomi.

A shallow bond of only one generation. Our parents were all born elsewhere. Those ravines, those caverns of leaves, I can't claim to be from anywhere else. I shush through brittle leaves in my sleep.

Today I'm wondering about what went on at the party. Is it because I've climbed out of the ravines for good? That now, at least in theory, I'm one of the dolts at some party I'm not even invited to? That it's me now wandering from conversation to conversation, hovering by the table with the hors d'oeuvres, shoving deviled eggs in my mouth so I don't have to talk to anybody . . .

Vanessa Baron huddled in a chair, comfy, barefoot, nodding off. It's late and there's just a few stragglers left, my parents included, and a ring has formed around her. And though she's basically comatose, Vanessa remains an adept hostess who somehow knows the precise moment to murmur appreciatively at one of the men's jokes or a half-told story.

The image has its roots, I believe, in something my mother

once said to my father as we drove home one night from Les and Vanessa's, my brother and me muddy and rank in the backseat.

"And," my mother said, "the whole time she sits there like a queen."

"I wouldn't say that. Perpetual princess. I'm not sure Vanessa will ever graduate to queen."

"She's mousy," my mother said.

My father didn't respond, which spoke louder.

Eventually my parents stopped going to the parties. And at some point, the parties, too, stopped altogether. Les and Vanessa, like everybody else, got divorced.

What happened to Les and Vanessa Baron?

I'd like to make something more of the swingers rumors but all I've got to go on is stale thirdhand innuendo. My bet is that even then, in the suburbs, my parents and everybody else's parents went home drunk and exhausted to their own beds, and that the idea of swinging was an early party fantasy rather than an end-of-party reality. Besides, what would they all have done with the swamp monsters who'd emerged from the ravines?

Only a little remembered decadence from the 1980s. Vanessa Baron slumped in a chair at the end of a night like some sad drunk in a John Cheever story. That big white house on the edge of the ravines, all lit up. From down in the ravine, it looked like an ocean liner at night.

In those early years, my parents must have congratulated themselves. This is why we migrated, why we left the soot, the noise, the culture, the Art Institute, the bookstores, the restaurants. *Think of the space! Good public schools! Free! No crime! Trees! Look at all these trees!*

The waiters in bow ties, circulating with their silver trays hoisted above their heads. I think of how the waiters came north from the city on the Saturday train. I remember being on my bike by the Chicago and Northwestern station and watching them step off the train already dressed for the night in their white shirts and bow ties. Paradise has got to be staffed. None of it would have existed without them, no green lawn, no tall trees, no charming drunken loneliness drooped in a chair.

» **9** «

On the cover of Gina Berriault's posthumous collection of stories and essays, *The Tea Ceremony*, there's a photograph of the author sitting in front of her typewriter. She's looking away from the typewriter, her barely open eyes are downcast, her thumb and forefinger tugging on her lower lip, as if she's trying to think of a word. There's a stack of books beside her. She's looking away from these, too. On the wall, what looks to be a drawing of an upside-down tree. You'd think it was staged but something about the distance in her eyes makes me believe she's working over a sentence in real time. There's a patience in Berriault's sentences that could only be the result of a refusal to rush any one of them into existence. The photograph captures an intensity of contemplation that's almost too intimate, not unlike the throb of her stories. In a rare interview conducted five years before she died, Berriault talks about Gogol's "The Overcoat":

> There's a description of the poor copy clerk's coat, how the cold wind got in across the back. I don't know why those lines move me so much, except when you visualize how the cloth has worn out without his knowing until suddenly one day he's surprised by that cold invasion—isn't that a description of an entire life?

27

What to say about an observation that penetrates into the soul of a story with such a simple question? Only that this morning I'm trying to isolate, visualize, as Berriault says, the instant when the cloth had worn away so much that the clerk first felt the cold. Hadn't he been feeling it all along? What was different about that particular gust that suddenly distinguished it from every other cold wind in the clerk's life?

I return to Berriault's fiction because of the way she distills a moment. The story that gave her final book its title, "The Tea Ceremony," is set in California. All Berriault's stories are California stories but she never worked an obvious angle. Her territory is the margins, the periphery, and her people are the ones who find themselves left out, not just of any sham California dream, but left out, period. We're in a small, dusty town south of Los Angeles. A teacher, Miss Ferguson, enacts a Japanese tea ceremony before her sixth graders. She's chosen the prettiest girl in class to assist and the two of them will go through each detail and gesture, slowly. Before they even begin, Miss Ferguson and Jolie Lotta admire the teapot, the delicate bowls, the bamboo whisk, all of it.

> They spent a minute doing that, Miss Ferguson making chirping sounds of belief, of belief in the beauty of the objects before them.

I can laugh at Miss Ferguson and her ludicrous chirping and yet I also recognize her near-fanatic faith in beauty. Such faith in beauty, and beauty alone, is always doomed. But who hasn't fallen for it? Miss Ferguson herself acknowledges that the Japanese, the people who gave us this exquisite ceremony, also bombed Pearl Harbor because they, too, are human beings and human beings, she says, are by nature treacherous.

Delia is not, and will never be, the prettiest girl in class. She imagines, horror of horrors, that dainty, elegant Miss Ferguson drops by her house unannounced.

> She'd know the worst if she came at supper time. Her suspicions about us, and I knew she had some, would be confirmed before her eyes. Other families sat down together, while each member of my family ate apart. A family askew, a family alone in a rain-stained bungalow in the weeds, faded curtains that didn't fit the windows.

Anyone who comes from a tattered family will recognize this scene. A family askew. And the fear that one of the Miss Fergusons of the world will catch us in our natural habitat. What? You people don't eat at the table? I conjure this paragraph so often that it's almost become untethered from the story itself—paragraph as island, as disembodied refuge—and, every time, I take my plate of food to some unoccupied corner of that rain-stained bungalow and chew slowly, listening to the sound of my own fork scrape my plate.

In our house we did eat together, if also alone, at a round wooden table so small our knees touched. It wasn't for lack of a bigger table. We had a long one in the dining room nobody ever went into. I've written about the kitchen table before. It isn't true that we write stuff out of us.

If my family could have scattered to various corners of the house on Hazel Avenue we would have. Our curtains were measured to fit the windows perfectly but that didn't matter, either. We sat at the kitchen table, night after night,

PETER ORNER

squeezed. And we tried to eat with as few movements as possible because anything could set my father off. A lazy burp,
a dropped spoon, a hiccup. This is nothing out of the ordinary. Tyrannical fathers are a dime a dozen in books and
neighborhoods. Ours was a little tomato-faced volcano in a
three-piece suit. Cutting up his steak, drinking his Schlitz
fresh chilled out of the freezer. There's no head of the table
at a round table. Maybe this sort of demarcation would have
made it easier, given us somewhere for our eyes to avoid.
There's no escaping a circle. My father, my mother, my
brother, and me. We're still wedged in there because there's
no greater fantasy on the face of the earth than the linearity
of time. Time only circles. We chew, we swallow, we try not
to call attention. The house is gone, flattened, bulldozed, and
we're still trying to make it through dinner.

» 10 «

Mr. Sandy drove a small brown car, an upright two-door Dodge, like a little hat with wheels. Lessons were at 6:30 on Wednesday nights. This went on for a couple of years. I had no competence or interest. The piano sat in the living room facing the front lawn. Mr. Sandy and I spent a lot of time looking out the window. It was either dark or getting dark, depending on the season. We came to an unspoken agreement. He'd mostly doze in a dining room chair while I'd sit at the piano and, every once in a while, doodle a few notes here and there.

"Twinkle, Twinkle" I could play, badly, or the beginning of the slightly more advanced "My First Waltz." A forgettable, unassuming man with a heavy, ruddy face, Mr. Sandy would sit next to me on that dining room chair dragged, by me, into the living room every Wednesday night. Big glasses hid his eyes. He'd prop his hat on his knee. I think of his knee, how his knee wore his hat. My mother, exhausted from substitute teaching, would be making dinner in the kitchen. Occasionally she'd bang a pot and then be very quiet so as not to disturb the lesson. She must have wondered why there wasn't much piano playing. Maybe she thought Mr. Sandy and I were, in low, serious tones, discussing music theory. When Mr. Sandy closed his eyes behind his glasses, I looked out the window at the lawn, at the graying light, at one squirrel chasing another squirrel. Like my mother, Mr. Sandy also came in the door exhausted. Afternoons and into the evenings, the man drove all over the North Shore giving lessons. I knew I was doing him a favor by not demanding anything of him. There must have been a time when he had a passion for the music. I can still play "My First Waltz" in my sleep, the opening notes anyway. You start with the middle C and radiate up the scale, hitting each subsequent note once before landing your thumb back at C.

I'm hoarding scraps. Sometimes, when I'm on the highway and about to run out of gas, I turn off the radio and the air conditioner, thinking this will buy me a few more miles. As if I can coast on the silence.

As a substitute teacher my mother didn't teach much. She told funny stories about my brother and me. The time he poured detergent on my head and locked me in the washing machine. She was very popular. She'd walk in the door and the kids would cheer. *Mrs. Orner!* But all work, no matter what it is, is tiring. My mother, in the kitchen, heartened by a few notes out of the piano in the living room. It didn't matter to her that it was only the beginning of the same song, over and over.

» II «

A TEN-YEAR-OLD BOY COMES HOME FROM SCHOOL AND
finds his mother gone. He walks to the nearby park and finds
her passed out under an orange tree. Her face is a ruin. He's
unable to shake her awake. It's not the first time. He decides
to wait beside her until she wakes up on her own. The speaker
of this poem—Robert Haas or not Robert Haas, what does it
matter?—supposes, looking back, that he must have wanted
it to look as though the two of them had been on a picnic and
that his mother had simply nodded off in the warm sunlight
amid the scent of the orange blossoms. And himself, just a
boy daydreaming beside her. How fast a kid learns the art of
the cover-up. You work with the scene you find.

  I keep threatening (to myself) to stop talking, remembering, describing, repeating, feeding off other people's words,
whatever it is I'm doing. Why not just let this be? Let a kid in
a poem wait beside his mother. How rare to just shut up. To
watch the snow out this window. Not the falling snow, that's
over, the snow that's already sitting out there, gone gray in
the street from the tire tracks. It's November 2019, or maybe
it's December already.

WOOOOOOOOOO, I HEAR LAUGHTER IN THE RAIN, WALKIN'
hand in hand with the one I . . .

Neither of my parents feel anything but it's impossible to listen to Neil Sedaka's jolly inanity without at least noticing you aren't feeling anything. Highland Park, 1976. They're in the living room. My father has made a fire. They're sitting in those two puffy white chairs. What happened to those puffy white chairs with the seat cushions that always reminded me of bloated stomachs? My brother and I aren't in the house. We're outside at the end of the street where the pavement drops off at the bluff. Below us, the lake. We're cold, or about to be cold. We listen to the lake swash in the dark without speaking. The two of them by the fire, the hi-fi on, the radio, WLS. Those two white chairs facing each other. Between them a chessboard nobody ever uses. My mother is looking at my father's left ear. My father is looking at the corner of a painting just above my mother's left shoulder, the abstract painting my grandmother didn't want. One day my grandmother brought it over and told my mother she couldn't stand it. *It's just brown slashes, what do I care how famous the artist is?*

My brother called the painting "Shit Storm over Lake County." My mother hung it in the living room and never thought about it again. How it goes with what we put up on the walls of houses, apartments, the places that we know sooner or later we'll leave; in my mother's case she was hoping sooner. In the meantime, you put things on the walls. What happened to "Shit Storm"?

"Catchy," my mother says.

"What is?"

"The song."

"Is it?" my father says. Catchiness isn't something he's ever thought much about. The fire pops, pops again. Then there's that fizzy hiss, as if the fire is exhaling.

My mother listens for the back door, for us.

» 13 «

SOMETIME IN HIS TWENTIES CÉLINE MADE HIS WAY TO
America, broke and meandering. From New York he took
the train to Detroit and got himself hired at Ford. He'd heard
Ford would take anybody, and this turned out to be true.
They took him. He did some job on the line for hours, what
it was he wasn't exactly sure. Something about calibrating
linchpins. When he proved incompetent, they gave him a little cart with tools to push around the factory. After work,
he found a brothel, because when you're Céline you find a
brothel. You want, Céline says, to get to the root of the trans-
actional nature of man? In any city, any country, go to a
brothel. By the end of the week, he's a regular. In *Journey to
the End of the Night*, he writes:

> To survive, I needed lecherous tonics, drastic
> elixirs. In that house I didn't have to pay much,
> they gave me friendly terms, because I brought
> the girls a few little refinements from France.

When higher-paying customers come around (baseball play-
ers, he says, carried around wads of cash), he retreats to the
kitchen to write stories. It's an image I like, the young Pari-
sian medical student, cold observer of our habits and hypoc-
risies, writing short stories at the whorehouse kitchen table.

He falls in love with a prostitute named Molly. Love's the wrong word. But there's tenderness. Also, he says, Molly's got amazing legs. Legs, Céline says, are the mark of aristocracy in humankind. Molly, saintly Molly. She pays him, not the other way around. She can afford it. She rakes in at least a hundred bucks a week. They take trips together to the outskirts of the city, to tiny lakes up in northern Michigan. Molly suggests, gently, that they could make a go of it. We could start a little business. Sell something. Candy? Open a deli? We won't be unhappy, she says. We'll be like other people.

As repulsive to him as being like other people sounds, Céline's tempted to stick around for a while longer. Molly. Oh, Molly, sweet, leggy Molly . . .

He rides the tram through the night. He leans his forehead against the window and looks out at this American city called Detroit, a name these clowns pronounce so incorrectly it hurts his ears. Still, it's what he sees. It's what Céline notices while riding that tram, the people who've been working all night cleaning stores and offices—freeloader, sure, but he was out there watching life. They're too tired to complain, he says of these people, because they've been reduced to meat.

And, as the sun begins to rise, he writes:

> On pavements sticky with the small rain of dawn
> the daylight glistened blue.

The Jew-hating shitbag he became deserves maybe a spoonful of posthumous forgiveness for giving us "the small rain of dawn." Don't we know the rain he's talking about. The sort of rain that's hardly falling but soaks you to the bone anyway.

» 14 «

My grandfather, my father's father—we called him Poppa—would sail around town in a rust-colored Lincoln Continental, doors big as Rhode Island. A suburban banker with an enormous planet of a head, a flag-waving patriot, a navy veteran, Ford-Dole sticker on his bumper—a brash, noisy man. Not an especially talented banker. He was routinely fired as a vice president of one suburban savings and loan only to get hired as a VP at another a few weeks later. A hail-fellow-well-met sort of guy. People liked him. He made a point of being well liked. The fact that he was liberal with the loans had to have helped. Outwardly jovial to the world, he wasn't a happy man. His wife, my grandmother, didn't love him anymore, maybe she never had.

He'd come home from a long day of giving money away without proper fiscal constraints and I'd be lying on the floor of the living room, the Cubs on WGN. My grandmother wouldn't be home yet from teaching a dance or exercise class or wherever she was. Still, Poppa would breathe, *Lorraine? Lorraine?* He'd call for her like that even though he knew she wasn't home because her car wasn't in the garage. I think of how he'd sigh *Lorraine* like it was the first word of a song to which he didn't know the rest of the words. He'd wait, as if he thought she might suddenly materialize in the doorway of the bedroom they shared and didn't share. Separate beds.

Hard as concrete. Jump on them, you'd stub your toe. Then he'd look at me and say, Where is she?

I'd shrug. Beats me. The studio?

Her last class ends at two thirty.

Hairdresser, then.

She had her hair done on Tuesday.

He'd leave again, peel out of the driveway, and roam the streets. People would be out on their lawns, and they'd say, Hey, that's my banker, Sy! Hey, Sy!, and they'd wave and Poppa would jam on the horn in acknowledgment of their gratitude for his largesse, and onward he'd drive. Once, he hit a kid on his bike, sideswiped him with the passenger-side mirror and the kid fell into some bushes. At first it was a hit-and-run. My grandfather sped around the block and came upon the whole situation in a new light. *For Christ sake, kid, are you all right?* Turned out he was, just a couple of bruises, and bruises heal, and my grandfather was a good Samaritan. It's how you get along in this world, he'd say, you got to seize every opportunity by the throat, steal a lemon, suck that free juice right the hell out of it. The television in the living room of the house on Pine Point Drive was a colossal Zenith, all white, more like a modern sculpture than a TV, and when he'd come home from driving around he'd sit there in one of my grandmother's plush pink chairs and concentrate on the commercials. When the game came back on he'd dispense life guidance. *Get a haircut. Learn Spanish. If they're taking over the country you may as well be able to talk to them. Get a haircut.* Over the years, he mellowed, shrank, became frail, lonelier, meek. His sweater vest hung off him like the ghost of someone else's clothes. *Grow your hair,* he'd say. *What's it matter?* He's been dead for twenty-four years. It occurs to me that in the scheme of things twenty-four years isn't that long to be dead. He's a youthful dead? Is this consolation? Maybe he's signing off on loans in another dimension? As I say, people liked him, he had a lot of friends. Everybody knew Sy. All he was looking for was his wife. He never seemed to find her. In the later years, she'd come home and stick something frozen in the microwave for their dinner and they'd eat in silence at the glass table in the kitchen by the window. In summer, when it was still light out, sometimes he'd point out a bird at the feeder, and she'd nod, yes, a bird.

» 15 «

I'M FAR FROM LAKE MICHIGAN, OUR INLAND SEA, AND—
again—I'm thinking about what it was like when my brother
and I left the house at night and walked down the dark street
to the end of the block and climbed the fence and sat perched
on the edge of the eroding bluff (dry, cracked, crumbling
muddy cliff), the lake down there in the autumn dark. How
the lake had a volcanic sound, the low roar of the waves so
constant that after a point we stopped hearing it, or thought
we stopped hearing it, the way you don't notice your own
breathing. Something so intimate about the noise of the
lake. My brother and I not talking. Whatever was happening in the lighted house behind us down the street or not
happening—nothing worse than the seething silence of our
house—whatever had driven us outside, irrelevant for the
moment. Nothing touched us, not even the cold. At least for
a half hour or forty-five minutes until we began to feel the
cold in our feet.

Of course Lake Michigan lacks the grandeur of an ocean.
That's the point of it. Lake Michigan is the sum of its lim-
itations. On a map it's a tear rolling down the face of the
Midwest.

To Walt Whitman the sea was never a static image. He
referred to it as that curious lurking something. Every time
he looked out at the water he saw it differently. The sea never

41

exhausted its possibilities because its motion never became specific. And maybe in a way my brother and I felt something like this on a smaller scale, even if we never would have thought it or said it, to each other or to ourselves. What we craved was motion, even at night when we couldn't even see the lake, as if the solidity of the house itself—the furniture, the piano, the couches, love seats, chairs, heavy dressers, beds, all the beds, all that lack of motion—was the root of our family misery.

I'm not after a particular instance of us out there. I'm trying to get at the idea of being on the bluff above the lake with my brother. How we never huddled together but instead occupied our own space in the cold, in the wind.

You want to go home?

Okay.

What?

I said okay.

We'd sit a few minutes more, waiting for the other to stand up.

Ready?

Sure.

I'll go when you go.

Fine.

So go.

Gimme a second?

You just said.

Don't talk.

» 16 «

THIS PAST WINTER, 2021, SEARCHING MY LATE STEP-
father's books, I find a copy of Isaac Bashevis Singer's story
collection *Short Friday*. It's a movie-tie-in edition. Barbra
Streisand's on the cover in Hasidic drag. Who knew my
stepdad was a fan of *Yentl*? He was a lawyer, a politician, a
former state representative and mayor. He read biographies
of Churchill, De Gaulle, Adlai Stevenson. His favorite writer
was Arthur Schlesinger. But who knows? We've all got our
secrets. Some of them are the books we leave behind. I sat
down in his old brown leather chair, the one that's in the corner of the den, the one we've all been avoiding. *Avoiding* isn't
quite right. Say we're leaving the chair open for him. Every
morning, before anybody else woke up, he'd be there in his
bathrobe, at his feet a pile of six newspapers, *The Wall Street
Journal*, *The New York Times*, the *Chicago Tribune*, the *Sun-
Times*, the *Waukegan News-Sun*, the *Highland Park News*.

A weary rabbi is in synagogue at dawn. He arrives early, before the few morning congregants, in time to watch the sunrise through the windows. Each and every dawn he has the
same thought:

Unlike the sun, man never renews himself though
he is doomed to death.

This particular morning another, maybe even more ordinary revelation comes to this worn-out rabbi in a place that
exists, now, only in geography known to the dead. I para-
phrase: *It's only the rich who make trouble! The poor never
scheme against me. They don't have the time. They're too busy
working* . . . This includes the few men who at this moment
are shuffling into the synagogue—Leibush the carter, Chaim
Jonah the fish merchant, Avrom the saddlemaker, and
Shloime Meyer, who has orchards outside Yampol . . .

What do we do with a rare moment of absolute clarity?
Most people, rabbi or not, do nothing. We put our shoes on
and go back to work. We return to ineffectual complaining.
In the rabbi's case, he might also have gone back to chastis-
ing himself for his ineptitude, his lack of proper rabbinical
temperament, his tendency to wallow in his lack of respect,
his desire to get the hell out of this stupid little town, his
hunger for a more prestigious appointment . . . but not
today.

Singer's "I Place My Reliance on No Man" is a minor fantasy. What if we gave up coveting? What would happen if we
genuinely renounced success and everything associated with
it? Just let it go?

The rabbi takes Shloime Meyer aside and asks him if he
needs any fruit pickers.

There's never enough fruit pickers on the face of the earth.
I'd like to begin tomorrow morning.
Pick fruit? But you're the rabbi.

The rabbi resigns his holy office and by sunrise the following day he and his wife and daughter are out in the fields.

We never hear how the wife and daughter feel about it. I'd give a lot to have heard that conversation.

Fine, fine, Mr. Salt of the Earth, but you have to drag us out here with you?

There's gossip, hell yes, there's gossip. Did you hear it? Rabbi's picking fruit! But it dissipates. Soon enough, there's a new rabbi for the rich to complain about.

Something else about this story. I'm not sure how it connects to the rabbi's decision to leave his pulpit. But it comes to me now. I didn't make a note of it at the time. The book is back on the shelf in Chicago, next to Schlesinger's *The Crisis of the Old Order.* It's about ghosts. That morning, just before the rabbi makes the decision to change his fate, there's a line about ghosts who pray. When the living Jews depart from the synagogue in the evening, Singer tells us, the ghosts take over. They remain all night, praying. And these dead souls scatter only when, just before dawn, the rabbi unlocks the door to the sanctuary. I remember, a few weeks ago, sitting in my stepfather's chair and thinking this makes sense. That after we die, we go on praying. Or maybe this is when some of us start?

17

EVEN MY GRANDMOTHER (WHO, AS A DANCER, APPRECI-
ated the choreography of boxing) knew Ali couldn't beat
Larry Holmes in 1980. He was too old, too slow; Ali in
name only. The saddest things were his legs. Motionless as
tree trunks. A man who used to dance. They say he needed
the money. Blame Don King and his hair combed skyward.
Couldn't Ali have done something else to raise the cash?
I only wanted it to be over. When the bell rang to end the
fourth, just before the commercial break, Ali retreated to his
corner, but he didn't slump down on his stool. It was like
Holmes had jabbed him to sleep on his feet. He seemed to
have no idea where the stool was. I wasn't the only kid who
believed he was doing this for me. Sure, there was a fat check
waiting for him whatever happened, but he was sacrificing
his body for me. A dumb Jewish kid, I'd absorbed the Christ
metaphor like everybody else.

Sunk in the big black leather chair in the den, watching, not watching, trying not to watch, hands over my eyes
peeking between my fingers. Ali's cornermen push him
down by the shoulders to the stool and just before the cut to
commercials—his face. More disinterest than weariness. The
kind of indifference that comes with being bone worn out. It
was long past anything to do with physical tiredness.

Save him, I begged Purina Cat Chow.

Round 5, 6, 7, 8, it no longer matters, and you'd think Holmes would start to take it a little easy but Ali's making twice as much, win or lose, and so Holmes has a point to make. Holmes wasn't a great fighter, which captures the essence of a final truth. Eventually, mediocrity beats the shit out of everyone. Holmes was a workaday heavyweight who'd once been Ali's sparring partner, so there's poetry in it, too. Ali of course understood this, given his genius for being all things to all people. The hired help is champion now. As it should be. I don't believe Ali ever begrudged Holmes the beating. A dull fight, what I allowed myself to see of it. Ali held up his gloves to protect his face and Holmes almost gently swatted them aside and clobbered with the same overhand right to the head again and again—and again. And then it became a thing, after every round Ali would retreat to his corner but he would not sit. It was as if to give in to his knees now would have meant remaining on that stool forever. His standing there like that was a lot worse than the fight itself. His cornermen shouting, cajoling, pleading—Sit down, Muhammad! Please! Please!—but he was no longer capable of hearing anything. I could tell this from Chicago, alone in front of the TV in the den. There may have been other people in my house but I was alone. And I wanted to whisper in his ear, Mr. Ali, even my own brother won't talk to me. And also fuck Don King.

The last thing I remember after they stopped it was that the ring was mobbed by all the people who loved Ali, including Larry Holmes. The victor struggled against the tide of bodies to get to Ali. Because even Holmes wanted—desperately, beyond desperately—to confirm those wounds were real.

18

I KNEW I'D NEVER READ IT. THAT NEVER KILLS THE craving. It's about my hand. It's about needing the spine in my hand. Community Thrift on Valencia Street. It was $1.25. Most books were only a dollar but if something looked interesting sometimes they'd tack on an extra quarter. You know the sort of book? One you buy just to hold? Then stick it on a shelf even though you'll die before you get around to reading it. Still, when the time comes, you box it up with other books, the read, the unread, the never to be read, and carry them all from one rented apartment to another rented apartment.

This past weekend, for no reason, I noticed it. It's a thin, jacketless hardcover, easy to miss. It was crammed next to one of those Updike novels about witches in the suburbs. (Never read that, either.) Euthanize me before I alphabetize. I need to be unable to find what I'm looking for. I pulled the book out, sat down on the floor, and read a little. It opens with Monet, up before dawn:

> The sky was still dark when he opened his eyes
> and saw it through the uncurtained window. He
> was upright within seconds, out of bed and had
> opened the window to study the signs.

•

Light is only an idea, an expectation. He hasn't much time. He needs to bathe and have breakfast as quickly as possible. This isn't as easy it sounds. Getting Monet out the door, I soon learn, entails the hustle of numerous servants. The woman who serves him breakfast, the man who rows the painter out to his little island studio, etc. It's clear that Monet was a pain in the ass—demanding of the servants, indifferent to the existence of his family—but what's alluring about the book's opening is that you start to feel impatient, too. Cook the egg already, woman. Can't you row this skiff faster, sailor? What he's after is not the sunrise itself. In fact, when the light does arrive, when it seeps through the trees over the edge of the horizon, it wrecks the scene completely. What Monet wants is that fragile fraction of time just before the sun begins to lighten the trees.

Too often I wake up late, after promising myself I'll be up early, and even then I'm almost too tired to face the morning light. I've never believed in books as forces of healing. As much as I live for them, breathe for them, they are only, for all their sometime glories, bound paper and glue. Maybe this is a clue to their power, the fact that they are so physically unassuming. At the end of any day, packed on a shelf, one looks like another. Think of bodies in a morgue.

Light by Eva Figes. It's ninety-one pages. I'm on page 17. I have no idea how Figes came to write this. The book jacket is lost forever, and there's no author's note, thank god. I don't know if Figes read biographies of Monet or stood in a museum and, for hours, studied Monet's paintings. Did she visit Giverny and take notes? Probably, she did all these things. But at a certain point, I imagine, Eva Figes, whoever she is or was, must have gone out in the blue predawn unlight and simply breathed. Light as plot, light as story.

Soon dawn would come, and with it would go
this hush, this cool luminosity coming through
stillness.

Only to slow down the arrival of morning, that's all he wants.

WHILE SICK AND BEDRIDDEN IN PARIS, RICHARD WRIGHT began to write haiku. After so many years of sentence after sentence, paragraph after paragraph, book after book, there must have been something about the compression that lightened the burdens he'd always carried. Before his death, he wrote more than four thousand haiku.

> That abandoned house,
> With its yard of fallen leaves,
> In the setting sun.

In 1983, Mrs. Felstiner drove her station wagon into the garage, shut the door with the clicker, and then climbed over to the passenger seat. The Felstiners lived around the corner and three doors down. There were two kids: one was in my class, Jacob; the other, Leo, was younger.

I remember she had very short hair, shorter than mine. My mother said it was the style. Mrs. Felstiner drove the car pool twice a week. She listened to the news on the radio. Once, she called for quiet and tried to explain to us, in the six-minute ride to school, what the Cold War was. I can't remember what she said.

After three or four days, Jacob was back in school. Outwardly, he acted like nothing happened. But I'd watch him during class. He'd be concentrating on the door in the middle of science and I'd think, he's waiting for her to walk through it.

When we laughed we checked ourselves and stopped. In the cafeteria we ate more slowly, without shouting at one another. This didn't last long. What she'd done soon became a fact. Once it was a fact, things returned to normal. But I'm talking about the brief time before that happened, when what she'd done was still floating, when it hadn't yet settled into a story of that year. We used to play this game, kill the guy with the ball. Jacob, who was taller and stronger than any of us, had always played it mildly. Even after, he still played it mildly. He always preferred to be the putz with the ball, not one of us, the ecstatic killers. We'd pummel and we'd pummel. I was waiting for Jacob to crack, to rage, or at least kick a locker or a fifth grader. It never happened, and in this, like so many of my stories, nonstories, there's no movement, no forward momentum. Jacob Felstiner, who's living somewhere and working, like anybody else, is still staring at the door during fourth-period physical science with Mr. Torgerson.

Richard Wright's daughter once said that, toward the end of his life, the rhythms of her father's haiku seemed to match the rhythms of his own short breaths.

Not long after, the Felstiners, what was left of them, moved away. The house sat empty for months.

» 20 «

MY FATHER CALLED THE NOISE MY BROTHER MADE A hocket. If my father liked the sound of a word, he'd repeat it. *Chartreuse, horseradish, gulag.* What my brother did was hocket. *Hocket* was a noun and a verb. It was something between a cough and a throat clearing, and my brother made this noise from roughly the beginning of the Ford administration, through Jimmy Carter and the bicentennial, and into the first few years of Reagan, and every time he did, between two and three thousand times a day, my father would shout, "Stop that hocketing!" which only made my brother hocket more.

Even now whenever my brother clears his throat I brace myself.

During what you might call the heyday of the hocket, say 1978, my brother had a turtle. I forget this turtle's name but my brother was very devoted to it and he, the turtle, was very devoted to my brother. We referred to the turtle as he but I'm not sure we had any idea. How do you tell with a turtle? In any case, whenever my brother hocketed, the turtle would stick out his head. It's an image I'll die with. There's that signature phlegmy e'hem—it seemed to emanate way back in my brother's throat—and his turtle's head would shoot out from its shell as if to applaud.

Once, I staked them out. I crept into my brother's room in

the middle of the night and waited for him to hocket in his sleep. When the hocket came, a thin, sleepy hocket, I flicked on the light and there it popped, his sad old wrinkled head, those green-brown, startled eyes. He was a vigilant turtle. A turtle with his own mind. He's a turtle with individuality, my mother would say. He's a real character. He'd eat peanut butter off your finger, and long after the peanut butter was gone he'd still be nibbling your finger with his teeth. I remember how much I loved the feel of those searching, daggery little teeth.

The turtle lived in a fish tank that my brother had decorated with drawings of weeds to make him feel at home. He didn't feel at home. He liked it under a bed. He liked it when my brother put him in the toilet for a swim. And he loved carpet, any carpet, but the snow-white carpet in my father's room was a particular favorite. A kind of pure landscape for a turtle to roam.

By then my mother was sleeping in the guest room. My brother and I were as vigilant as the turtle, alert to all sounds. Every creak, every sigh. Knockings, murmurings, pleadings. My mother in the guest room reading, a bar of light under the door, and my father turning the doorknob and finding it locked.

Rhoda?

One day the turtle shat, happily shat, on my father's carpet, a runny shit that stretched from the closet to the big bed. Our attempts to rub it out with Ajax only made it multicolored. When my father came home from work my brother begged/hocketed for clemency. My father was thrilled to issue a pardon with the caveat that if that swamp creature crapped on the carpet again he'd put the little green fucker in the Cuisinart.

The inevitable. Why does it always come as if from nowhere? The afternoon my brother liberated him from the tank, put him on a rug, and hocketed hello. Nothing happened. My brother hocketed some more. Even I tried my bad imitation of a hocket. Nothing and nothing. He was so close to us, you know, right there, and yet hidden. We knew we'd never see that wrinkled head again. Unless we cut him open, I suggested. But my brother ruled against it. He said no hocket autopsies. Out in the backyard we dug a little hole. No shoebox, we thought he'd appreciate the soil more. My brother's eulogy. You were an exemplary amphibian hocket. You were steadfast and your devotion hocket will never be forgotten hocket hocket. There should be more to say. We knew this day would come hocket as you were old, ancient really hocket and yet we thought we'd have more time with you. Well, you've gone to a better place hocket at least in theory hocket but how can anybody know for sure? You know. Now you hocket know. And yet you remain in the darkness of your shell hocket, your ancient scuffed house. Amen.

» 21 «

IN ROBERT HAYDEN'S "THE WEB," THE POET, BY CHANCE, brushes aside a spiderweb. Hayden contemplates the spider's point of view and describes how it dangled for a moment, "aerialist hanging / by a thread." I pause here on this sudden suspension. One moment you're minding your own miraculous business and the next thing you're dangling over the abyss. Now, you could argue that spiders are more accustomed than most creators to this sort of disaster. How often must it occur?

For fuck's sake. Again?

For the last hour, I've been rereading this brief poem. I've started to feel it in my gut. How quickly an exquisite web becomes wreckage, a fit snare, Hayden writes, for nothing but his own:

Embittered thoughts

These embittered thoughts give rise to a comparison. The poet thinks about another web, one more intricate and fragile than the one he's so casually destroyed. This other web, the one created in the poet's mind, is, paradoxically, stronger and a lot less elegant than the spider's, and not so easily annihilated.

Rereading, grasping, I wonder if Hayden means to suggest

that this other web is a trap we walk around in and call our lives. We can't spin anything. We plod forward. Some days are good, you hardly notice. Others days are tougher. Still others are even worse. We think we can't go on. Of course, we can get out. There is always a way out. The fact remains that most of us don't take it. Most of us stick around, for better, for worse, for the duration. Is this because, knowing the end of our story—no matter who we are—we're still curious about the particulars of our individual deaths?

In an essay, Robert Hayden once praised reticence as a supreme literary value. I understand this to mean that there's truth in hesitation, in not rushing headlong into certainty, into pronouncement.

A commonplace enough thing to do, to break apart a spiderweb. I see the poet outside among the trees in the early morning, pausing to think about what just happened. Hayden doesn't provide any external details, not time or place, and nothing at all about whoever is speaking. He doesn't need to in order for me to see the scene. He ends "The Web" this way:

> Caught in that filmy
> trap, who shall
> contrive to escape?

Each time I read it, this poem slips further out of my grasp. But maybe this is where I need to be, snared, dangling, groping between getting it and not getting it.

I don't think by "contrive to escape" Hayden necessarily means suicide. I wonder if he's suggesting there's no breaking free at all from the confines of our lives. That no matter what we do, action or inaction, the flimsy but infinitely durable trap remains intact. Live with it, don't live with it, it's there.

It's December 2020. I'm in White River Junction, Vermont, in the small room I rent in the old hotel here. It's early, not many people around, aside from the essential freight workers shouting to one another in the railyard across the street. We're on lockdown. I shouldn't be here. Don't tell the governor. There's never been anything essential about me. Each time the freight cars are coupled, the whole building shakes. As I read Hayden, I wait for them, these great crashes.

» **22** «

MY MOTHER HAD A FRIEND WHO'D BEEN MARRIED THREE times. She'd come over and they'd talk at the glass kitchen table. (On Hazel Avenue, this table had been part of the patio furniture.) This was after we moved out of my father's house, now we called it that, to a rented house on Oak Street. On Hazel Avenue, my mother never had friends over. On Oak Street every door was always open.

My mother and her friend would sit in the kitchen, drink wine, and laugh. I'd join them. I was twelve and loved gossip. They never seemed to mind that I was there listening so intensely to whatever they were going on about. Being married three times, even in the '80s, that triumphal era of divorce, was rare and my mother's friend wore it proudly. She was rich, each of her husbands was rich, but even so she wore the money lightly and went to work every day as a social worker in Evanston. Working didn't seem to tire her out the way it tired out my mother. What I'm trying to remember is something that my mother's friend carried around with her, an unspoken thing, which is that Richie, her oldest son from her first marriage, died in an accident. He fell into a sewer shaft while playing frisbee down in Urbana. I'd never met him. My brother says he looked like Jim Morrison. Even when he was alive, my brother says, Richie Levy looked like a myth. It was one of the ghost stories of my childhood, what happened to Richie Levy. I'd try to imagine what that fall—apparently someone forgot to replace the manhole cover—must have been like. One moment you're loafing after a drifting frisbee in the wind, the next you've dropped into a void. I remember watching my mother's friend for signs. I tried to hear in her laughter, in her distinct low smoker's cackle, what? The fall itself? The silence that followed?

She used to howl, my mother's friend, at how long it took for my mother to leave her first husband. My mother, for years, agonized over it, how it would scar us kids, etc., etc. She'd point to me: *Does this head full of ears look scarred?* And she'd say, *My God, Rho, you've got your whole life—*

Mid-Morning

your outrageous forgetting & remembrance,
your ghosts & rebirths . . .

—YUSEF KOMUNYAKAA,
"Nighttime Begins with a Line by Pablo Neruda"

I'M ON A BENCH IN A LITTLE LEAGUE DUGOUT. MY DOG IS pissing on third. There's a lot that's deathlike about the geometry of baseball. You start at home and if you're lucky you round the bases and return home. If you're not lucky, same thing, only quicker. Either way, you end up back here in the dugout. In the center, equidistant from all the bases, forty-six feet from the plate, a mound of dirt rises like a year-old grave. None of this has anything to do with Kafka. I do know that he liked sports and used to work out naked in front of his bedroom window. He also said in a letter to Felice that he didn't want to be a hermit, he wanted to be dead. He wasn't suicidal; he thought being dead would improve his concentration.

Visionary readers are, by their nature, generally unknown. Because these readers—the few that exist or have existed—for the most part turn their pages in clandestine silence and rarely share their thoughts in print, or even out loud to anybody.

I'll posit here in this empty dugout that Kafka, rarest of ducks, was an incomparable reader. I'm talking about the person who wrote a single paragraph about *Don Quixote* that breaks open like a blossom.

Kafka says that it was Sancho who invented Don Quixote. That it was Sancho, the sidekick, who created the character for his own amusement, as well as a kind self-exorcism. That it was Sancho—Sancho!—who expelled the devil from his own brain by letting loose a complete lunatic upon the universe. A funny, moral, courageous lunatic who has the audacity to descend, literally, into fiction itself. It took three hundred plus years of people reading the novel for an insurance adjuster who lived with his parents to read it (in German translation) and reveal what had been in front of everyone's faces all along. Sancho's pulling the strings. Why else would *he* be the one unable to fully immerse himself in fantasy? Not only does Sancho have less fun but his bruisings and clobberings are no less real for having been invented, more so because he, Sancho, unlike Don Quixote, actually feels the lumps. This is the price you pay for being the wizard. And yet the genius of Sancho is that nobody ever suspects it's him telling the story. Often, even he forgets.

I can see Sancho at his desk, his quill flinging across the parchment.

Only a reader utterly emancipated from the clutter of other people's ideas could have concocted a theory this unpolluted. The fact that Kafka apparently wrote the paragraph only for himself just adds to its splendor. He wasn't trying to prove anything to anybody. He was only talking to the walls after midnight, imagining Sancho imagining Quixote. In a few hours he'd have to be back at his desk at the Worker's Accident Institute.

It was Max Brod who found it after Kafka's death and gave the piece its title, "The Truth About Sancho Panza," and delivered it, against his wishes,[1] to the world. For this we owe

---

1   In this regard, though, I'm with Borges, who says that if Kafka truly wanted his work burned, he'd have lit the match himself.

Brod immense gratitude. But it must be said that the title messes with the spirit of the paragraph, as if announcing a secret revealed. The last thing Sancho wants is to be the center of anybody's attention.

Something else about this empty diamond. Maybe it's the short brown grass and these bases like the flat uniform headstones that remind me of an Orthodox cemetery on the northwest side of Chicago. Aunt Gert is buried out there. A scabbled field with stone markers flush with the ground. A place that forbids adornment of any kind. No flowers, no pagan good cheer. Death no party, say the rabbinate.

And I think of all dead readers, not exceptional ones, just ordinary dead readers of the sort that you and I will become. The kind of people who, after reading a certain sentence, might pause to think for a moment or two before moving on. What if these thoughts, your stray thoughts, my stray thoughts, don't vanish? What if they remain in the atmosphere? When a thought comes to us out of nowhere, what if it's one of these disembodied scraps?

» 24 «

WE HAD A NEXT-DOOR NEIGHBOR WHEN WE LIVED ON
Oak Street who used to wander into our house through the
always-open front door. Mr. Aiello was a little man in an
undershirt, and when he stood in the front hall, his chin
lowered so that it touched his throat, he looked even smaller,
child-sized. Sometimes he pressed up against the wall or
nuzzled among the jackets hanging in the front hall closet.
He'd be murmuring to himself, an urgent murmuring. The
way he spoke into his chest like that made me think he was
ashamed of whatever it was. I'd wake up in the middle of
the night and head down to the kitchen for some cheese and
there Mr. Aiello would be, moving his lips fervently in the
dark. Mom, I'd shout, and she, groggy in her nightdress,
would walk him slowly home, arm in arm. He got agitated
when either my brother or I got too close. But my mother
calmed him. In her presence, his shoulders loosened.

Oh, Mr. Aiello, my mother would say, nice of you to
drop by.

He was a Korean War vet who'd for decades run a successful construction business and was known as no nonsense; a tough old fuck is how I once heard him described.

The Oak Street house bordered Fort Sheridan. We could
see the double-barbed-wire fencing of the army base from
our yard. I remember reading once that Fort Sheridan was

built after the Civil War to protect Chicago. Protect Chicago from what? An attack by some socialists from Wisconsin? (A dated joke; there used to be a lot more socialists in Wisconsin.)

My father would call the house every night. The phone would ring and ring until finally my brother would pick up the receiver and stuff it in the silverware drawer. My father would say hello, hello, hello, hello in the dark to the knives and forks.

Who knows what news Mr. Aiello was trying to convey? Suburban Elijah, this one came to prophesy only to himself. For some reason he needed to do it in our house. My mother was kind to him, which became part of the ritual. It's possible that's why he came in the first place, so my mother would be the one to guide him home.

» 25 «

THE MYSTERY OF WRIGHT MORRIS ISN'T WHY HE'S SO forgotten, it's that he was ever much known in the first place. Because it's true that Morris was, if never a household literary name, at least mentioned among (need it be said?) the mostly male literary heavyweights of his day. All told, between 1942 and 1986, Morris published thirty-three books, including novels, prose fiction, books of photographs (what he referred to as photo-texts), essay and story collections, and memoirs. A Nebraska native, Morris spent much of his life in northern California remembering, and reimagining, the Midwest.

Forgotten, yes, but still among us. There will be no splashy Wright Morris revivals. No tale of a bestselling novelist stumbling across one of his books at a yard sale in Schenectady and raising him from the dead. Morris has remained in print all these years, thanks to the University of Nebraska Press and not the bigger houses that used to publish him: Knopf, Harper and Row, Scribner. Each let Morris go after poor sales. When Viking brought out a *Wright Morris Reader*, hoping to do for Morris what a portable compilation of greatest hits did for William Faulkner, the editor wrote, "We, who look forward to each book of his as it is announced, and talk about it with excitement when it appears, cannot understand why so many pulses remain calm."

And in spite of a long list of appreciators that includes

Eudora Welty, Ralph Ellison, Saul Bellow, Maxwell Perkins, Wallace Stegner, Rosellen Brown, Charles Baxter, and Michael Parker, pulses have never much quickened to this day. Morris specializes in Midwestern oddness. He's drawn not to what makes us homogeneous but to what makes us strange. Morris's people, even when they are staunch conformists, aren't quite like anybody you've ever met. They aren't like anybody *they've* ever met, either. Morris, I believe, woke up every day thunderstruck at the variety of human existence—in Nebraska alone.

As much as he was interested in people, Morris was equally obsessed, in both his prose and his photography, with what he saw as the populated emptiness of abandoned spaces. Rusting farm equipment, old shoes, discarded clothes, yellowed mattresses—all were stories left behind. He once wrote, "What is it that stirs you about a vacant house? I suppose it has something to do with the fact that any house that's been lived in, any room that's been slept in, is not vacant anymore."

I've got many of his books. *The Works of Love, The Field of Vision, Ceremony in Lone Tree, Cause for Wonder, Fire Sermon, A Life, Love Among the Cannibals, One Day, My Uncle Dudley, The Fork River Space Project* (which asks the question: Did Fork River, Kansas, disappear in a cyclone, or was the entire town abducted by aliens?) . . . but I always come back to his last, *Plains Song*. It's as if Morris needed to write eighteen other novels before he could write this one. The subtitle of the novel is "For Female Voices." There are men in *Plains Song,* but they aren't especially relevant.

Sharon Rose's mother is dead. Her father is as distant as his name, Orion. Her aunt Cora and her first cousin Madge live next door, just across the field. It dawns on Sharon Rose early, as it dawns on so many of us, Are you kidding me? I belong to these people? It's not possible. Still, it is Sharon Rose's bond to Madge that grounds her existence. Growing up, the girls are inseparable, cousins in name only. As the two get older, Sharon Rose feels betrayed when Madge becomes interested in boys. After Madge becomes engaged, Sharon Rose shrieks at Madge, "Is he looking for a wife or a housemaid?" Aunt Cora overhears her and whacks the back of Sharon Rose's hand with a hairbrush. Madge calls out, in an act of generosity that catches my throat every time, "She don't mean it the way you hear it!"

Only somebody you've loved your whole life could muster this sort of understanding. *She don't mean it the way you hear it.* Sharon Rose flees the farm at the earliest opportunity, first to study piano in Lincoln, then Chicago. Eventually, after the end of an affair with a woman named Lillian Bauman, she takes a teaching job at Wellesley. But there's always Madge. Sharon Rose's desire to never look back is thwarted by an ache for Madge back in Nebraska and home that was never home.

I read *Plains Song* again this week. I read it to remind myself, again, because I have forgotten again, how the things I think I'll be able to hold on to, my family, my young kids, my work, will be outside of my grasp soon enough. The bewildering inconsistency of time. In this book certain moments last pages. Other times, the years pass in half a sentence. Major characters suddenly become minor. People die mid-paragraph. Isn't this how it happens? Blink and you're forgotten. Sharon Rose's mother, Belle, the mother she never knew. Belle who came to the Plains from the Ozarks. Belle who brought such life and vigor to that farm, to that family of stoics. Belle who talked a blue streak and didn't care if anybody listened. Belle who had a habit of thrusting out her lower lip and blowing up to cool her face off. Belle who loved brown sugar and honey and costume jewelry. Belle who had spells of moodiness. Who used to wander at night. Belle. She lives for exactly eighteen and a half pages—eighteen and a half wild erratic laughing pages—before she vanishes from the book and from the history of her daughter's life. I brace myself when I reach this sentence on page 59: "Two days before Christmas, Orion was off somewhere, hunting, when Belle began her labor."

Can't she live this time?

» 26 «

Horses have gone lame
Crossing the waste lands
Between two people.

—DONALD JUSTICE,
"At a Rehearsal of Uncle Vanya"

MID-MORNING AND MY GRANDFATHER IS SITTING AT HIS
desk, his notary public stamp in his upper left-hand drawer,
alongside the pornographic comic books he brought back
from the war. I drank those comics into my eyes in gulps.
I also played with the notary stamp. You held it by the two
scissor handles and squeezed. I notarized everything, dollar
bills, toilet paper. I notarized ants, squeezed them to death
by the authority vested in me by the secretary of state of the
state of Illinois . . . My grandfather looks out the window at
the front walk. Nobody is expected today. It's a shame because my grandfather loved company. He'd shoot the shit
with anybody about anything. He liked to keep a conversation going, any conversation.

He'll be dead in a couple hours. At the moment, he's rest-
ful, calm. Whatever will make his heart cease just before
noon will have nothing to do with physical exertion. He'd
been reading William Tecumseh Sherman's *Memoirs—On*
the 8th all our troops reached the neighborhood of Clinton, the

weather fearfully hot, and water scarce. Johnston had marched rapidly, and in retreating had caused cattle, hogs, and sheep to be driven into ponds of water, and there shot down so that we had to haul their dead and stinking carcasses out to use the water. On the 10th of July—until his eyes drifted off. The book remains open in his lap, and now he's staring out the window at nothing in particular, at the flat-topped shrubs he's trimmed himself. It's early April and the birds have gone quiet. After he retired, he put all his Civil War memoirs in alphabetical order by general. *Grant, Longstreet, McClellan, Pope, Sheridan* . . . There's a gap where Sherman's book should be. We could use a word for that. The space on the shelf where a book used to be. A hollow? There's no word for an empty grave, either. He also neatly organized, by date, the letters he wrote from his own war. He wrote my grandmother a letter a day for the three and half years he was in the Pacific. I found them stuffed in a plastic green Marshall Fields bag (*Marshall Fields* in frilly white script) at the back of his closet when, years later, after my grandmother's death, I helped clear out the house for the estate sale. The letters were rubber banded and arranged by month and year. In them, he often begs her to write him back, to tell him what's happening at home.

Please, Lorraine, can't you put pen to paper and write to me?

He's wearing those big glasses and the flare of the morning sun flashes off the metal frames. His wide forehead and perfectly round head. Not totally bald, he has a sheen of hair that covers his head in thin parallel lines because he spends time every morning combing them. He's not a vain man, he only wants to pay homage to what little he has.

My grandparents' rock-hard separate beds. Even so, he's always been close enough to reach her, touch her, across the dark.

My grandmother was a dancer, a showgirl. Throughout the mid- to late 1920s and into the early '30s, before she
eloped and had my father five months later, she danced at the
Oriental Theater, at McVicker's, at the Panther Room. I have
a stack of her publicity photographs, another of my inheri-
tances. My grandmother, at nineteen, in a feather boa, bare
right leg raised high.

My dead look out windows. So many of these windows are
gone. I'm not sure it matters. 814 Lunt Avenue. 322 Fargo Avenue. 78 Pine Point Drive. 513 Hillside Drive.

10 July 1945

My Darling—

Another day and still no word from you— But I
suppose that last week this time you were in the
process of moving— I know how busy you must
be— How is everything working out—are you
satisfied at all— Do you think you will like it—
I'm so worried that the house is going to be too
much for you and that you won't like it— I hope
I'm wrong— Please write and—

My grandmother is taking a shower. He can hear the
water running. And he thinks, vaguely, of her body and
how he used to hunger for it, the water streaming down her
shoulders.

» 27 «

ELLEN, AN EIGHT-YEAR-OLD, REMEMBERS THE DAY A man knocked on the door and asked her mother if she could spare any old boots. It was raining. It is usually raining in Maeve Brennan's Dublin.

> He was all wet, and his eyes were full of rain. Ellen thought he might be blind but then she saw it was only that he was all wet, and the rain was so straight and heavy that even at this short distance it fell like a curtain between them.
>
> —"The Beginning of a Long Story"

It's raining today also, in White River Junction. A cold early March rain, and it's pecking the windows like somebody's down in the alley throwing pebbles.

Ellen's mother has no boots to spare. The rain continues to fall. She invites the man inside for tea and to warm up a little. She serves him tea. Also Ellen's mother gives him dry socks. Then she leaves him in the kitchen. This seems like a bad idea. Just a mother and three young girls alone in the house. But all this man does in the story is fall asleep at the kitchen table, his teacup in front of him. You know the way a person sleeps when they're so tired nothing else matters?

Ellen spies on him as he lies there huddled over the table, arms wrapped around his head, hiding his face. After a time, the man begins to shout in his sleep. Ellen stands in the kitchen and watches him.

> She wanted him to be quiet, as he had been, and she thought that if she stared at him he would be quiet, or wake up, but the words came out growling and roaring and bubbling in a voice that was much too fierce to belong to the poor little man who lay wet across the table . . .

I can't explain why I find "if she stared at him he would be quiet" so moving. Some kind of mood I'm in, this rain, the empty alley down below. No one's throwing pebbles. A little girl watches a strange man rage in his sleep and thinks that her eyes alone might bring him relief. It must have something to do with the way Brennan resists the need for any direct verbal communication. The man doesn't suddenly wake up and see the kid and mutter a few indelible words that an adult Ellen will later remember. A rare thing to purposely avoid the sort of combustion that occurs when characters play off each other. For Brennan an eight-year-old staring and believing that this alone might help a stranger is enough. She lets a drenched man who needs sleep, sleep.

» 28 «

JODY CRENSHAW TERRORIZED US. IN THE 1980S EVERY school had to have a bully. This was a point of pride. There had to be someone whose role it was to kick the shit out of you for no reason. Jody Crenshaw, Jody Crenshaw, Jody Crenshaw. At recess he'd lurk in the tunnel that connected the school with the fields on the other side of Sheridan Road. You had to run a gauntlet in the dark. If he caught you, he pummeled you. Put you in a headlock and pummeled you. Make it past him and you're a hero but at the same time you're missing out. It's like I've reached a stage where everything must be consecrated. I have a friend who once said that I practice a form of nostalgia that borders on hysterics. Jody Crenshaw? He's luminous, also? I only remember him outside, never inside any classroom. He didn't talk, he grunted. He had facial hair, nearly a full beard in seventh grade.

My face in the wet nodge of Jody's sweaty armpit.

There was a light in the tunnel. Whenever the custodian replaced the bulb, Jody would punch it out with his fist. What he did had to be done in the dark. He wasn't discerning. Jody played no favorites. Bodies he wanted, nobody's in particular.

» 29 «

Dear Mrs. Engerman,

You did what you could with me. I was slow. Others weren't. Melanie Gurewitz, for instance. She said Hester Prynne represented the nascent rise of first-wave feminism. I thought about Hester in ways you wouldn't want to know. Melanie Gurwitz would have slugged me. I live in New England now. I thought I'd celebrate my annual descent into depression (November to June) by reindulging, after all these years, in puritan-flavored sin. And I've got to say my reread was fairly consistent with how it was back when you gave me a charitable C+ based solely on my vigorous class participation because I turned in no work. In my post-high-school experience, sin has always been worth it. Hawthorne still rains on the parade. He doesn't—forgive me, Mrs. Engerman—give us much sense of Hester and Reverend Dimmesdale's copulation. For Hawthorne, all is aftermath. Their moment of presumed sexual congress is so fleeting it hardly happened while it happened. Now, this I know pretty well. Tiny spasms of undiluted rapture—followed by? What? Hawthorne's right. It's all aftermath. I've become solemn, Mrs. Engerman. You spent a lot of fifth period talking about symbols. You weren't dopey about it, and you encouraged us not to be, either. The red letter, you said, wasn't so much a symbol of adultery as it was a representation of what everybody in the village believed was the demon inside them all. Hester was only the embodiment of the message, and we all know, you said, the role of the messenger. She brings the news nobody wants. *Hester is us*, you said. *We are Hester.* Who wants to hear it? Who listens? (A case in point: to this day, nobody names their kid Hester.) At the time, all this was over my head. It wasn't over Melanie Gurewitz's, obviously. I'm trying to reconsider, or as you once said, "resee."

When Dimmesdale, that lameass, that overdramatic hypocritical coward—Dimmesdale is worse than Chillingworth any day—walks out into the night, he finds himself on the scaffold where, years ago now, Hester had stood to receive her judgment. As he's standing up there, who joins him?

> And there stood the minister, with his hand over his heart; and Hester Prynne, with the embroidered letter glimmering on her bosom; and little Pearl, herself a symbol, and the connecting link between the two.

Even in 1850 *bosom* must have sounded asinine. Mrs. Engerman, I'm not trying to turn in my final essay (Introduction, Body, Conclusion) thirty-two years too late. You wouldn't accept papers even a minute after fifth period started. Not that this would have passed, either. It's only that I noticed something in the "Minister's Vigil" chapter, nothing earth-shattering, it's probably in the Cliff's Notes, but I thought of you, Winifred. Can I call you Winifred? Hester and Pearl aren't there. Dimmesdale's halluci-nating. And yet they are there, right? Because that's how it is with hallucinations. What isn't there is there. Visions are things. And as the three of them stand on the scaffold, holding hands in the dark, this lit-tle nonfamily of three, Pearl asks Dimmesdale, "Wilt though promise to take my hand, and mother's hand, at noontide tomorrow?" And Dimmesdale, because even when he's hallucinating he is a chickenshit, says: "Not then, child, but another time." And Pearl, savvy kid that she is, laughs in his face. But this moment, great as it is, isn't what really got to me. It's what hap-pens just after. Hawthorne brings weather. A sudden meteor shower.

> The great vault brightened, like the dome of an immense lamp. It showed the familiar scene of the street, with the distinctness of midday, but also with the awfulness that is always imparted to familiar objects by an unaccustomed light.

People say you've died, Winifred. I refuse to believe this. Is it weird to say I felt your physical presence while I was reading? This might distress you, wher-ever you are. I'm a professor now. No PhD, let's not get carried away. I've a bogus degree known as an MFA. (A fun couple of years, kind of like art camp in the Midwest with New Yorkers.) The idea of seeing the familiar in unaccustomed light? It's not a tired

metaphor about seeing something in a new light. The
light is materially different. The night has, for a moment or two, become day. Arthur Dimmesdale, like
most of us, isn't anybody's idea of a swashbuckler.
Yet: the meteor shower does, for a moment anyway,
change everything and Arthur sees, the limpdick
sees.

> They stood in the noon of that strange and sol-
> emn splendor, as if it were the light that is to re-
> veal all secrets, and the daybreak that shall unite
> all who belong to one another.

I know you will have flagged, even from the grave,
Hawthorne's use of the word *noon*. He turns time itself into light. You may have mentioned it in class.
It's the sort of line that used to make you bop your
forehead with an open palm.

» 30 «

I CAME HOME FROM SCHOOL ONE DAY AND FOUND THE
front door wide open. At first I thought it must be our neighbor Mr. Aiello, but he only haunted us at night. I prowled
from room to room searching for clues, doing my Columbo
routine. I was scared witless when I reached my mother's
room and found that her jewelry box had been dumped
upside down on the bed, rings and bracelets scattered.

When my mother came home, she went through the mo-
tions and called the police. Two bored suburban cops mo-
seyed in with their fingers in their belt loops. They surveyed
the crime scene in my mother's bedroom. A single mom,
blond, perked some interest. *No man living here presently?*
She filed a report, which, I imagine, is still in a file cabinet at
the Highland Park Police Department.

My mother realized the obvious the moment she put together what had been taken and what hadn't. As in: the bur-
glar left valuable pieces and apparently took only those of
more or less sentimental value, such as a cheap pewter ring
that had once belonged to my father's grandmother. And
the wedding ring she'd retired months before—that too was
gone. She'd never miss it.

A minor episode, and one that the three of us, my mother,
my brother, and me, eventually forgot about. It wasn't worth
much thought. For a week or two maybe we locked the door.

My mother, in particular, didn't want to dwell on it. She was through dwelling on my father. Now that he was out of sight, he almost didn't exist anymore, and this, for her, was a blissful thing. And I can't imagine that my father really cared very much about some cheap ring of his grandmother's. Thinking back, it seems to me that his entering the house on Oak Street, the only time he ever did, had more to do with the fact that we'd moved on, though we were only a mile and a half away.

My father had expensive tastes. The house on Oak Street must have struck him as a dump. My mother did the best she could, she'd had to furnish it fast. She'd taken a job in the city, at McCormick Place. She hardly had any time at all. Not that furniture had ever mattered to her. Our mismatched sofa and chairs. The fake fireplace. All of it, everything was unfamiliar, ours and not his. I think of him tsking over the coffee stains in the carpet. The whole house was covered in once-yellow shag, stomped and flattened by previous renters. My mother had it steam-cleaned but the stains remained. There's a cliché that I've always been drawn to. Water under the bridge. I think not just of the water but of all the other shit in the river, the flotsam. What a beautiful, accurate word. The robbery itself was, that year, nothing but flotsam.

My father standing in my mother's bedroom in the spring of 1987. The indentation of my mother's head in one of the pillows. All his rage and sorrow and humiliation and loneliness. My brother thinks that I've gone easy on my father in print. That I'm rewriting a pathetic history in order to cook up some counterfeit redemption.

» **31** «

JAMES WRIGHT HAS A POEM ABOUT A GOAT AND HIS
aunt Agnes. It's got a pretentious title, "Ars Poetica—Some
Recent Criticism." It's never put me off. A goat has escaped
from a carnival and some boys are trying to stone the poor
thing to death. Small-town Ohio, sometime in the 1930s. The
goat attempts an escape down the alley that runs behind
Aunt Agnes's house.

> And my Aunt Agnes
> Who stank and lied,
> Threw stones back at the boys . . .

And she protects it, gathers that goat up in her arms.

Years ago, somebody I loved, a person with a bona fide
PhD in English, once said that not only is James Wright out
of style and irrelevant but his particular brand of mawkish
backyard sentimentalism is regressive. And okay, harsh, but
it's not like I don't get it. Aunt Agnes is used, she's romanticized. The poet, while underscoring how much Agnes stank
and lied, how repulsive and loony she was, of course makes
her the savior. Isn't crazy Aunt Agnes's degradation poetic?
Isn't it lyrically powerful?

Now lock her up in an asylum in Cambridge.

Not that Cambridge, the poet says. Cambridge, Ohio, you moron, which is "no more Harvard / than you'll ever be."

A nice touch, this Harvard stuff. Funny. But oh, did Agnes stink. Her house stank, too. Wait a few more decades, then stick her in a poem with a pompous title.

> I gather my Aunt Agnes
> Into my veins

Why this sudden hunger to defend Wright to somebody I no longer speak to, as if this argument wasn't as buried as 2003? And Wright? He drank himself to the grave in 1980. Scoff all you want, but I love the poem for what it says, what it fails to say—and what it refuses to say, which is, as I see it, that the motivations behind love, any and all love, are always suspect, if not always corrupt. But what else have we got? What's the alternative? Deny the existence of love altogether? It was seventeen years ago, no, eighteen now. That doesn't mean it didn't happen.

Agnes, she never received a kind word from anybody, not from her husband, her children, not even from her nephew, the fucking poet. Still—still—every time, she rescues that panicked goat, pulls it close with her sloppy arms.

» 32 «

HOWIE BAUMGARTEN WAS ONE OF THOSE PEOPLE WHO
returns to his hometown because it's the last place that will
have him. Having failed every other place, where else is
there? Not that anybody in Highland Park would have cared
much if Howie Baumgarten dropped dead in the street wearing one of his homemade tie-dyed shirts.

He opened up a store on Central Avenue and Second
Street, where Chandler's Stationery used to be. Howie's place
was filled with cheap, random stuff nobody wanted. We'd go
there after school and not buy anything.

Also, Howie had a monkey. I forget the monkey's name.
With that gaunt little monkey on his shoulder, Howie spoke
in sudden, spastic bursts. His voice was so high it was like
he'd sucked up the helium he used to blow up his balloons.
The man could monologue and breathe through his nose
at the same time. You don't realize what a feat this is until
you try it. When Howie talked his monkey listened, his little head in profile. And then, without warning, as abruptly
as he'd begun, Howie would clam up, go completely silent,
and squint at us from behind his oversized glasses. Then
he'd watch us as we wandered around the store, picking stuff
up, putting stuff down. Shoplifter, Howie said, any one of us
rosy-cheeked nothings could be a shoplifter. The monkey
would watch us, too, like a hawk.

Gag gifts, dusty art supplies, magic tricks, knock-off Slinkys, Magic 8-Balls. He sold rainbow-colored afros. He sold goldfish that he scooped out of a dirty fishbowl with a spoon and dropped in ziplock baggies. Balloons, more balloons. Off-brand candy. Grow-it-yourself crystal. Shoes that farted. Any useless hazarai a wholesaler was trying to unload cheap, Howie would buy in the eternal hope that some person, someday, in some not-so-distant future, might drop two or three dollars on it.

"I'm not looking to get rich," he'd say, "I'm only looking to—" He'd squeeze a plastic dog turd that squeaked. "Get it? Get it? Eek by!"

Most of the time his speeches were about how he'd been ripped off by one supplier or another.

"These people are rapacious. You've got no idea what a small businessman in America endures, not a single clue. Tell your fathers, those paper titans, those captains of non-industry, those bilkers off the tit of the common man, what it's like out here in the harsh light of modern reality."

"My dad sells lumber," Mickey Ross might say.

"Proletariat of the world unite! We'll hang all the fathers, each and every one of them, by their toes like Mussolini. We'll start with the lumber barons. History is circular, don't forget. What goes around comes— You think if you shit on people you won't get shat on? That it only flows one way?"

"He works at the Ace, Howie. He doesn't own it."

Then, without transition, Howie would bolt right into a few rousing thoughts about how even so things were getting better every day, a little hunkier dorier, that we'd be surprised how many old ladies came in for the costume jewelry.

"The biddies spend all the money they squirrel away on the earrings. They pay me in quarters and nickels. They shake out their coffee cans on this very counter, the savings of a lifetime. Isn't everybody entitled to a little beauty? I'm in the dream business. I hold up the mirror so they can look at their ears."

He didn't seem to have any family left in town. Or maybe they'd disowned him long ago. We didn't know where he lived. He may have slept in the back of the store. Whatever the case, he didn't have much, just the rented storefront and the things he worked so hard to collect. There was always new inventory. "Check out these magnets, they work on skin, it's a miracle, I'm serious, gimme your arm—"

Howie may have been an ordinary loser. But inside his store, behind his counter, he was king freak. That wild bramble of curly hair, his pealike eyes behind those giant glasses. The tie-dyed shirts that didn't fit over his stomach. The monkey.

Senior year, Mickey drew a cartoon of Howie for the school paper. In it, Howie, monkey on his shoulder, holding a festoon of balloons, floats away into space. I've been trying to remember what the caption said because apparently it was the caption, even more than the drawing, that set Howie off. He ranted for weeks. He said he'd been humiliated before the eyes of the world, as if *Shoreline* was *The Wall Street Journal*. Not merely personally insulted, but legally injured.

"Intentional affliction of emotional distress. It's a tort. Any of you fuckwads know what a tort is? *An act or omission that gives rise, directly or indirectly, to an injury or harm actionable in civil* —"

He wrote letters to the editor; he wrote letters threatening to sue Mickey, Mickey's parents, the school district, the superintendent, the city of Highland Park, the state of Illinois, the NFL, the League of Women Voters . . .

He banned Mickey Ross from the store. For life, he said, effective immediately. He put a poster in the window. His own cartoon of Mickey with exaggerated buck teeth, and under it: BANISHED IN PERPETUITY.

I call Mickey in Chicago. We still talk. He's one of the few people who answers the phone anymore. He couldn't remember the caption, either. "Some forgettable joke," Mickey said. He's had his own knocks. A rough divorce, in and out of work, trouble with one of his sons. He never says what kind of trouble.

"You think I don't still feel bad about it? Last thing Howie needed was some smart-ass drawing a picture of him. You're writing about Howie?"

"What makes you say that?

"Why else would you call?"

"I call you all the time."

"Spare him the pity, the false amends."

"Jesus."

"Am I wrong?"

"I'm just trying to tell it straight, not make a character out of him."

"Right," Mickey says, "because he already was a character. You don't have to do any work."

"Do you remember the monkey's name?"

"He must be dead by now."

"The monkey?"

"Howie."

"How are you doing?" I said. "I mean really—"

"You're asking?"

"I called you."

"You called me about Howie."

"Mick."

A few months after the cartoon it was summer. College, followed by whatever we've done with our lives since. Eventually, Howie closed the store and reopened a few months later in Evanston, near Northwestern. He must have figured he'd have better luck with college kids. That store didn't last long, either.

I try to resist the temptation. Vanished people should stay vanished no matter how findable they've now become. He was just a funny dude we knew in high school. In the afternoons we'd hang out at his store. In a post dated February 12, 2020, Howie Baumgarten writes that he's in a spot and could use some help, any help. "I'm not particular. Cash, checks, PayPal. No longer accepting Diner's Club."

There was a single comment. It was from a kid I remember from high school, a year below us. "I always liked you, Monkeyman. Stay strong."

Nobody can hide anymore. Nobody even wants to hide anymore?

I call Mickey back. "Howie's not dead."

» 33 «

THREE IN THE MORNING AND NOBODY IN THE HOUSE CAN sleep. It's as if all three of them, a daughter, a son, an elderly father, separate in their beds, are suddenly awakened by a similar sense of dislocation. Without a word all three convene at the kitchen table, this humble center of the universe. Glory begins a makeshift breakfast. For her the ritual of stirring batter for pancakes is one way to get through this unplanned gathering in the dead of night. As if the simple fact of hot food might act as a kind of balm for agitated souls.

Yet another scene at the kitchen table in a book of kitchen table scenes. I don't have the novel with me. I'm on a bus just outside Manchester, New Hampshire, heading north on I-89. I've no book at all. My books are in the hold down below. Something about this mostly empty bus made me think of Jack and Glory and their father. Marilynne Robinson's *Home*. Another scene in a kitchen, and a reader might be forgiven if the scenes jumble in memory. The scene I am thinking of is unusual because it breaks a pattern.

Glory is making pancakes, but they haven't come together at the table for a meal. Her brother Jack hasn't been back in Gilead for very long. Maybe a couple of weeks at this point. After twenty years (the amount of time Odysseus was away from Ithaca) he is, finally, home in Iowa. Jack is no Odysseus. He's only been down in St. Louis. I'm also not sure calling him prodigal would be accurate. In my dim recollection of the parable the prodigal son squanders his inheritance. Though it depends on how you'd define inheritance, it's clear that Jack didn't have much to squander, at least in a material sense. Brains and charisma, sure, these he's still got, even in his current ragged state, but they aren't going to buy him lunch.

We don't know why he's come home. He must be on the run from something. Even an ordinary failure can do a hell of a lot of damage, and that damage often involves the cops, the law. It wouldn't be the first time he's been locked up.

Or: maybe there isn't any specific reason. There are times when your feet simply gravitate homeward.

It's a wordless scene, if I remember, and it culminates— and this is as vivid to me as the stark pines that line the interstate—with old Reverend Boughton slumped in his chair, fast asleep. Jack scoops up this once formidable man and ferries him back to bed. Like I've done countless times with my own daughter, and now my son.

The three of them will wake up in a few hours groggy and anxious. This isn't a family to sleep late, even Jack. Nothing is solved. But Glory, who's recently returned home herself, watched her brother carry her father. It's a beginning, of what Glory doesn't know yet, but it's a beginning.

Another moment comes to mind. Whether it is before or after the kitchen scene I can't say. Reverend Boughton demands of Jack: "Let me look at you. When you were a child you never stopped long enough to let me look at you."

My own father used to demand this of me. Sometimes he'd even plead it. Hold still, won't you? Let me look at you.

» 34 «

MY MOTHER AND I WAITING ON LINE TO SEE THE KING
Tut extravaganza at the Art Institute. How giddy we were to
see all that treasure. The line snaked down Michigan Avenue
to Van Buren, across the street from Roosevelt University,
where my uncle Milt once took classes and never graduated.
I daydreamed in the July swelter. When the line moved, I'd
fail to notice a gap that had formed. My mother would nudge
me. She's always believed in the importance of keeping your
place in line. Together we edged closer to Tutankhamen. Uncle Milt was my grandfather's much younger brother, nineteen years younger. He'd divorced at forty and a couple of
years later was found floating facedown in the Chicago River.

He didn't make much of a success, my grandmother said
of Milt.

The Tut exhibition wasn't at the Art Institute, it was at the
Field Museum. I stand corrected while at the same time be-
wailing the tyranny of accessible facts. (I plant my toothpick
flag on the landfill of inaccurate memory.) And since the exhibition was at the Field Museum, the line would never have
reached across the parkway to Michigan and Van Buren. It
most likely would have stretched eastward, in the direction
of the Adler Planetarium.

Also: Tut was in November that year, not July.

We couldn't have been sweating, my mother and I, we'd

have been bundled like babushkas. It must have been some other time, that July time on Michigan Avenue, waiting for some other blockbuster show I no longer remember. Herein ends any and all connection between King Tut and Uncle Milt. It wasn't even tenuous, it was as far as the Art Institute is from Roosevelt University, across the street and down the block, but as far as the hoity citadel of purchased culture is from a working-class college. Not only is my memory bad, I lack imagination. There's nothing at all between them now, the teenage pharaoh buried with lots of golden junk to give him a leg up in the underworld and an unlicensed bean counter (Milt never got his CPA) laid to rest in his best cheapish suit.

» 35 «

MAEVE BRENNAN WAS ONE OF THE GLAMOROUS ONES, one of the stars of *The New Yorker*'s heyday, from the mid-1950s to the end of the '60s, and one of the few women staffers. She wrote stories as well as the "Long-Winded Lady" columns for Talk of the Town. There was nothing long-winded about the long-winded lady. Brennan's New York street pieces are always concise, never bloated. She holds back just enough so that a reader becomes complicit in any given scene she describes. She evokes, then beckons you to join her and see it for yourself.

> The bewildering snow gave the shabby street an air of melancholy that made it ageless, as it will someday appear in an old photograph.

The simultaneity of time present, future, and past, bagged in a single sentence. I look out the window of this room I rent in White River, at the empty brick building across the street that used to be a phone company, and I try to see it differently, imagine the long-gone bustle. A roomful of operators talking into headsets. I love the idea that in order to talk to someone you had to first ask someone else.

Brennan can animate a place—or a person—with awesome speed and economy.

> He was very handsome except for his nose, like
> Marilyn Monroe's nose was indefinite, and
> blurred almost to thickness.

Again, she yanks me into her way of seeing. I've got to slow down, let the fully formed image take shape in my mind. A handsome somebody with an indefinite nose (Marilyn's!) blurred almost to thickness.

Brennan never walks her streets thinking she's above anybody else, not her readers, and never the people she observes so intensely. In a "Long-Winded Lady" from the mid-'50s, she describes a man in a supermarket trying to decide, with the little he's got, whether to buy a can of beans, a whole canned dinner, a can of soup, or canned chicken à la king.

> He had thirty-seven cents or twenty-nine cents or
> some sum like that, and he was standing there
> with the four cans, glaring down at them and all
> around at the stalls of vegetables and fruit and
> bread and so on.

By the beginning of the '70s, after the publication of her first book of stories and the disintegration of her marriage, Brennan began to lose her grip. Alcoholism and mental illness, always lurking, began to take full hold.

Her biographer, Angela Bourke, writes with compassion about Brennan's life after that point. In and out of cheap hotel rooms, institutions. When she felt good, she went off her medication. Occasionally hell broke loose, like the time she smashed all the windows of a colleague's office. Sometimes she slept in *The New Yorker*'s women's bathroom. (Likely a private spot, as she was one of the few who used it.) But much of the time, it seems, she disappeared into the streets. She no longer wrote very much although every once in a while she'd send a new piece to her editor, William Maxwell. The magazine also continued, in that old-school way, to pay her regularly. Bourke writes in *Maeve Brennan: Homesick at The New Yorker*:

> She brought a sick pigeon in from the street and nursed it there, and when she got her pay cheque she would cash it at the Morgan Guaranty Trust on the corner of 44th Street and Fifth Avenue, then stand outside, across the street from the office, and hand out cash to passers-by.

She died in a New York nursing home at the age of seventy-six in 1993. If I lose this already tenuous hold, may I stand outside the West Lebanon, New Hampshire, branch of the Ledyard National Bank and give away money I don't have.

» 36 «

I THINK OF THOSE FEW TIMES WE ATE IN THE DINING
room of my grandparents' house on Pine Point Drive. The
dining room was connected to the right side of the kitchen
through a set of swinging doors. The tendency in that house
was always to go left out of the kitchen and into the large den
with the big windows. That's where life was lived, where the
TV was, where we played bingo, my grandfather hollering
like so much depended on B-15, G-54. He paid cash money
right out of the fat wallet that bulged out of his front pants
pocket like a growth. The dining room was reserved for birth-
days, anniversaries, Passover, and on these more formal oc-
casions, Ruth, my grandparents' housekeeper for forty-seven
years, would wear one of her wigs. Ruth had a platoon of wigs
in the closet of her small room off the kitchen. They lived on
Stryofoam heads on the upper shelf, a row of them, each a
slightly different hairstyle. I'd put one on and parade around
the house while Ruth said that she'd call her lawyer on me.
My father was her lawyer. I'd say go ahead and call him and
she'd say she would, that if I didn't think she'd call him I was
stupider than I looked in that wig. Plus, she had a pending
case against the Chicago Transit Authority and needed to
speak to her lawyer anyway.

On those nights we ate in the dining room Ruth would
come in and out the swinging doors in her wig, in her white

nurse's shoes, carrying dishes covered in tinfoil to keep them hot. And on those nights my grandfather would clear his throat and stand up and begin some patriotic speech or another and Ruth would groan, Oh Jesus, save us.

As a preamble, let me say that America is a fruit that lets us eat of it, that welcomed us, a bedraggled, exiled, hungry people, to open our mouths wide and—

Dead. All three long dead, my grandparents dead, Ruth Armstrong dead. Ruth had her own family, of course. She had no children of her own but her sister and brothers had kids and so there were nieces and nephews and grandnieces and grandnephews, and I remember being jealous when she talked on the phone with her sister. I'd pick up a receiver in a different room and listen in on all the family gossip. *Simone says she's in love again, and this time*— Then I'd pretend to be choking or I'd fall down the stairs or I'd let one of the cats out into the street.

But for Ruth, Pine Point was a mostly somber house. Vines crawled up the yellow brick like the place was trying to hide itself.

Ruth and my grandmother were close, though each, if asked, would have denied it. Their public stance was to disparage each other. My grandmother said Ruth did nothing but prattle on the phone all day. Ruth said not only didn't my grandmother know how to cook an egg, she didn't know where eggs came from. *She thinks they hatch in the carton.* But those two talked, through my grandmother's darkest times they talked, through the death of my grandmother's daughter, my aunt, they talked.

She knew my grandparents' desolation, their separate beds. She changed the sheets every Tuesday and Friday.

Weekends, she took the train to her sister's. On those two

days my grandparents had to fend for themselves. I could exaggerate and say they were hopeless. They weren't. They went out to dinner.

Of her own griefs, we knew very little. Once, though, in the late '50s, after she'd already been with my grandparents for years, Ruth left. She got married. Three months later, she called my grandfather and asked him to pick her up in Milwaukee. He did. He got in the car and drove to Milwaukee. Nothing else was ever said about it, as far as I know.

She wore her second-best wig to my high school graduation, the one with the wavy curls.

It isn't details, specifics, it's all the hours, the hundreds of hours we spent together in the kitchen of the house on Pine Point.

Grilled cheese?

Yes, please.

One or two.

Four, I want four.

Go wash your hands.

The little black-and-white TV on the counter, one of her shows on low. She liked soap operas and *Maude*.

When I was younger I'd sleep over at Pine Point and always, in the night, I'd squeeze into Ruth's narrow bed with her and the two cats. Those cats, I've forgotten their names. They were the ones who paid the price on weekends because nobody fed them.

All love is personal, no matter how off balance. After she did finally retire she moved in with her sister on West Madison. By then I was in college.

In "Those Winter Sundays" Robert Hayden asks, in lines that have not stopped ringing since I first read them: *What did I know? / What did I know of love's austere and lonely offices?* The refrain is a dirge for those who start paying attention only after the fact. What did I know? What did I know? About anything?

There was nothing austere about Ruth whatsoever—but loneliness? All those years out in the suburbs, Monday to Friday?

Only my grandfather attended her funeral. The rest of us were scattered. They only told me about it later. My grandmother thought even my grandfather's presence was inappropriate. She didn't say *inappropriate.* She probably only scoffed that my grandfather was always insinuating himself at funerals, needing to gladhand and be the center of attention.

For Christ's sake, if anybody's family, Ruth's—

Oh, Seymour, she worked for us.

» **37** «

ABOVE A LAUNDROMAT IN NEW BEDFORD. A CRAMMED, creaky-floored, undusted, sneezing, wheezing, natural habitat of books. Every available space on the shelves had long since been completely stuffed, and the books were jammed three rows deep, behind one peeped another and another. Books rose in teetering piles like stalagmites. Books blocked the window, the emergency exit. The only way to move forward was to creep along narrow, winding, precarious paths. One false move and you were flattened by a stack of Balzacs. From below, steam wafted up past the windows like smoke.

A pale, thin proprietor made it clear that he'd rather be reading than accepting my torrent of compliments. *Melville himself might have shopped—*

"Melville's in aisle five."

"How do you survive? I'd have thought a store like this would have long since—"

"Online sales."

"Oh."

"Can I help you with anything else?"

"Where's the rest of the fiction?"

"Everywhere."

•

I bought a single book to pace myself, pledging I'd return. I intended for the store to become a personal mecca, that, at least once a year, I'd make the pilgrimage to New Bedford whenever I was in Fall River visiting my dead. New Bedford and Fall River are sister cities. I haven't made it back. Sometimes eleven miles is too far. I don't have the heart to check if the store is still there.

It's a plain hardback with no image of any kind on the cover. Only the title, against a cream-colored background, laid out like this:

WIND AND BIRDS

AND

HUMAN VOICES

Beneath the title, in small letters: *Stories by Ellen Wilbur.* Published by Stuart Wright of Winston-Salem, North Carolina. Wright was a one-man publisher who was also, apparently, a chiropractor. I bought the book because it promised exactly nothing.

Imagine you're driving through a small town. It's raining, a downpour. Lights are on in the scattered houses. You're lonely, you've been driving for hours, if only you could take a little shelter in one of these well-lit rooms. Ellen Wilbur will not only bring you out of the rain, she'll hide you in the bedroom closet and leave the door open a crack.

> One night, two years ago when I made love to
> Mary, I could see she enjoyed it and wasn't doing
> it to please me the way she usually does. ("Ned")

We all know what goes on in our well-lit houses. Or:

> There were times with his hot breath on my face
> and his voice crying my name, I felt I'd be more
> comforted and serene if I were sitting there alone
> and free of all the yearning human arms can
> cause. ("Faith")

All the yearning human arms can cause. It's enough sometimes just to retype someone else's words.

As far as I know, *Wind and Birds and Human Voices* is Ellen Wilbur's only book. Since 1984, she's been silent, at least in print. I've never thought it my business to ask why a writer stops writing for other people. May as well ask someone why they stopped loving someone else.

The final story in the book is called "Perfection." It's five and a half pages in the mind of a woman who is talking, only with her eyes, to an acquaintance she barely knows across a crowded table in a restaurant.

> I wonder why people ever speak at all, when
> everything they say is barely an outline . . .

She tells this person across the table a story, without saying a single word, a kind of fairy tale, about a man who believed, with all his soul, that his true love existed though he had no evidence at all, only a certain image in his mind. One day, at a party, this mythical soulmate actually appears, on the arm of a husband. Aside from a brief moment of wordless connection, the friend, the dreamer, makes no attempt to interfere with the woman's life. It was enough to know she existed.

Eventually, the acquaintance gets up to leave. Nothing need happen in a story other than hunger. What's more potent than possibility? I remember a look that once came my way from across a room. This was in Somerville, in the mid-'90s. I had a potato chip in my mouth and I was reaching into the bowl for another when I happened to glance up at someone I hadn't met.

Hey.

Do you remember? Nothing came of it. Nothing needed to. The room, the light, the potato chips. Years ago now, and still—

» 38 «

PIER PAOLO PASOLINI CHAMPIONED THE LITTLE GUY, the honest poor, the people he called the lumpenproletariat. He never pretended to be one of them. His father had been a military officer. On the cover of my City Lights Pocket Poets edition of *Roman Poems* is a black-and-white photograph of Pasolini in a trench coat, sunglasses, and severely coiffed hair, walking through a Roman slum surrounded by smiling children as if he's a politician on an inspection tour. In "Sex, Consolation for Misery," he wrote:

> But from the world's trash
> a new world is born . . .

He may have romanticized the idea of poverty but he wasn't full of shit. A committed Communist (even after they tossed him out of the party), Pasolini always took the side of anyone who worked for a living.

In another of the Roman poems, "The Weeping of the Excavator," the poet watches money being counted:

> with lazy fingers by sweaty delivery boys
> against facades flashing by
> in the eternal color of summer.

I, too, I tell this room where I talk to myself. I, too, was a delivery boy. Pizzas. I delivered pizzas for Luigi Amalfitano, Pizza King of the North Shore. I make no claims to being part of anybody's lumpenproletariat. Still, didn't I deliver hundreds of pizzas? I often got lost, couldn't read the map, often arrived late. Nobody's happy to see a delivery boy bearing a cold half-cheese, half-pepperoni.

I'd take the cash but I'd never count it until I was back in my mom's Corolla. Only then, under the dome light, would I check to see if I got an extra two or three bucks. One frigid night, I delivered a pizza to Melvie Rosen, a business associate of my father's. Melvie lived in a huge house on the lake. He'd inherited a regional chain of muffler shops. There was a story about him. Melvie had once been kidnapped, plucked right out of his own driveway and held for ransom. I remember my father saying at the time, "Who'd want him? Who'd want Melvie?"

"Nobody," my mother said. "They want money, not Melvie."

After a couple of days he escaped out a bathroom window in Michigan City, Indiana, and for a week, in the early '70s, Melvie Rosen was a provincial celebrity. Fifteen or so years later, I delivered him a pizza. He opened the door with a book under his arm. A little man with a beard shaved into the shape of triangle. My father once said that Melvie considered himself an intellectual because he'd attended the University of Chicago and that he "eschewed" the muffler business even if it did buy him a mansion on the lake. He didn't know me from Adam. Why should he have? I was only my father's son, and my father was nobody, a low-level plaintiff's attorney who represented Melvie on a few chicken-feed cases. I took his pizza out of the warmer. He accepted it and, though it was a little awkward with the book under his arm and the pizza, he managed to shove a wad of bills into my palm. I stood there on the threshold. Without a word, he kicked the door shut. Anyway, the wad felt thick, and I remember walking back to the idling Corolla thinking, Jackpot. Me in the driveway of that lakeside enormity, all those dark and empty rooms, the heat blasting. Under the dome light I counted. Singles, fourteen of them, exact change. Melvie, you cheap fuck, I'm still pissed. My father was right, who the hell would want you?

Luigi, that pizza pooh-bah, paid us two dollars an hour. If delivery boys made anything, we made it in tips. I was a suburban kid in my mom's Toyota. Still, I think Pasolini would say that Melvie Rosen stiffing me wasn't nothing.

Pasolini was murdered in Ostia in 1975. Officially, he was bludgeoned beyond recognition by a guy he'd propositioned for sex. More likely it was a political hit. The powers that be had reason enough to want to knock him off. He'd been sticking it to them for decades.

Melvie was important enough to kidnap but not to murder, though I'll bet the kidnappers wanted to after they checked the bathroom and found it empty. Melvie sprinting down the street in Michigan City in his underwear. Last I heard, he's retired in Florida. If he'd given me a couple of extra dollars on a cold night in 1985 I'd have left him forgotten.

» 39 «

IN THE LAST FIVE MINUTES OF THE ALGEBRA II FINAL, I copied off Stu Pearlstein. Pearlstein was as stupid as, if not stupider than, I was. Mr. McCord pinched my neck with greasy fingers as I was leaning over Pearlstein's shoulder. He hissed, tuna breath in my ear, *Dead to rights, Ornery, I've got you dead to rights.* The next day my father made an appearance at school in his cashmere coat and cordovan leather shoes to bail my ass out because McCord wanted to flunk me outright and failing would, my mother said, ruin my odds of getting into a decent college—odds that weren't hot to begin with—and so in a rare bipartisan moment she enlisted my father to throw his weight around on my behalf. And my father, gleeful his weight could be of service, waltzed up the steps of the very high school he'd attended. I waited in Mr. Salke's office as my father in his elegant coat clacked down the hall toward us. Salke grinned at me. As vice principal in charge of discipline and academic misconduct he reveled in his role as both executioner and pardoner.

"This place is as dumpy as I remember," my father told Salke.

"Your tax dollars," Salke said.

I was then dismissed, simultaneously, by both of them. This was going to be mano a mano. I didn't care what happened either way but they must have come to some agreement because McCord ended up passing me with a D and eventually another mediocre student from the suburbs snuck in, through a back door, to a college of repute. Mr. McCord would have to be long dead, my father dead, Mr. Salke, most probably dead—my days are peopled by the dead—but I'm trying to understand something. If I was so indifferent to everything and everybody, why did I inch closer, closer, so I could peer over Stu Pearlstein's shoulder? The kid fisted his pencil like an ape. Some weird act of faith? Love? To put yourself in someone else's completely incapable hands?

» 40 «

THE LOMANS' BROOKLYN NEIGHBOR, CHARLEY, PLAYS the straight man to an increasingly unhinged Willy. There's some suggestion that the two men are related, which might explain how Willy's hostility toward Charley coexists so seamlessly with his willingness to ask Charley for money. He's family. We curse our people. Then we hit them up for cash.

Charley doesn't have many good lines. He's not pushy. He doesn't dream big. His son, Bernard, is a bookworm. Willy, on the other hand, swears by the American cult of being well liked. Willy tells his oldest son, the ex–football star, Biff, that things can't possibly go wrong if you're well liked.

> **WILLY:** Bernard can get the best marks in school, y'understand, but when he gets out in the business world, y'understand, you are going to be five times ahead of him. That's why I thank Almighty God that you're both built like Adonises. Because the man who makes an appearance in the business world, the man who creates personal interest, is the man who gets ahead. Be liked and you will never want. You take me for instance. I never have to wait in line to see a buyer. "Willy Loman is here!" That's all they have to know, and I go right through.

BIFF: Did you knock them dead, Pop?

WILLY: Knocked 'em cold in Providence, slaughtered 'em in Boston.

You know if you need to knock 'em cold in Providence, you've got a problem. It's impossible to believe that Willy Loman, even in his prime, was ever a good salesman. The entire play, he never once mentions what he actually sells. He made a living. That's the point. He didn't have to be great at selling whatever he was selling. Now that he's older, he can't pull his weight anymore. And yet because Charley is Willy's opposite—he's successful, modest, not a blowhard—he comes across as a thoroughly dull character. It's a relief when late in Act Two it's Charley who says:

> Why must everybody like you? Who liked J. P.
> Morgan? Was he impressive? In a Turkish bath
> he'd look like a butcher.

See the play live, this butcher line always gets a laugh at the very moment we need it. Because by this time Willy's desperation is almost too much to take. He's in retreat and inching closer and closer to the rubber hose he's connected to the gas line in the basement. And not only does the line redeem and enrich Charley's character, it also cuts to the chase.

Lovable losers abound in literature, but in life? The truth is we can't abide them. Never have. A loser? In this country of opportunity? And the last thing anybody will accept is a loser in the family. It's as inexcusable today as it was when *Death of a Salesman* premiered in 1949. About J. P. Morgan, Charley adds, after a pause:

But with his pockets on he was very well liked.

It's telling, isn't it, that while we all laugh at this, too, Willy doesn't. He's that far gone. Earlier in the play, Linda begs Biff:

Be loving to him. Because he's only a little boat
looking for a harbor.

Because Linda knows, has always known, that Willy's nobody. Biff is so pathetic, in part, because he's always half bought what Willy was selling. I always find myself wishing Biff had a less ridiculous name but his goofy, misplaced optimism makes the whole story deadlier. Biff's trouble is so obvious. A high school jock who finds himself lost and aimless in his thirties? Because he believed in all the cheers, in all that being well liked?

This morning I noticed something that had never caught my attention before. *Death of a Salesman* has a subtitle.

CERTAIN PRIVATE
CONVERSATIONS IN TWO ACTS
AND A REQUIEM

It makes sense; the play is made up of certain private conversations, most of which aren't between the characters. They're between Willy Loman and Willy Loman. There are ordinary-seeming scenes where characters talk to each other about the concerns of that particular moment, but always, simultaneously, there's this alternate conversation going on in Willy's head. It's not what I remembered. It's not about the death of any salesman. It's about the confusions of a fundamentally sapped human being. In the end, Willy talks in his head to his own long-dead brother, Ben. It's Ben who asserts the financial soundness of using the rubber hose. Pure American math. You are worth more dead.

» 41 «

AMONG MY MANY FALL RIVER UNCLES, HORACE WAS THE
well-heeled crook, an investment banker who bilked many
people, including friends and relatives, especially relatives,
and lived high on that hog for years. Turned out there were
few investments. The old con, robbing Peter to pay Paul: he
and his brother were only moving money around. When his
brother, Morty, the front man, the charmer, died in 1970, the
jig was up. Some of the larger investors received a portion of
the liquidated assets but small fries, namely relatives, people
like my grandfather, ended up recovering nothing. The story
goes that Grandpa Freddy had just discerned how broke he
was when he fell out of his chair, pen still in his hand. His
heart gave out. Under the last entry in his account book
blazed a single line in red that runs right off the page. He was
fifty-nine. His hand, my mother has always said, dragged the
pen across the paper as he fell.

Years ago, while on a bus in San Francisco, I wrote a
story about Uncle Horace. He returns to earth as a barefoot,
hunchbacked ghost on a bus. When I confront the ghost
about what he did to my grandfather and the others, Uncle
Horace responds, "I was loaded. They all wanted what I had.
I'm to blame? I'm criminal?"

The story is two and a half goofy pages. There's some more
conversation. A few more jokes. A little pathos. At one point,

the barefoot ghost helps a woman with her shopping bags as she climbs onto the bus. In the last line, after smooching the narrator's ear and stepping off the bus, the ghost inexplicably calls out, "Sayonara, turkeyboy."[2]

I sold it to my friend Oscar at the *San Francisco Chronicle*, which at that time, on occasion, because Oscar was creative, published fiction. My mother was proud to see me in a newspaper. She was convinced my career was finally taking off.[3] She sent it around to the family. Some, including members of my uncle's more immediate family, were less impressed. For a couple of weeks I received threatening phone calls and emails. I was accused of playing games with real lives to amuse myself—and to make a profit. One of my cousins, married to a guy who works at HBO, called and left a message on the answering machine saying that I'd never have anything of mine made by HBO in this lifetime or any other. "As if," she purred. Before she hung up, the kicker: "You're just as nauseating as your father."

Another person, a distant relative I hadn't known existed, wrote to say that, very clearly, I was echoing an angry rant I must have heard from my grandmother Sally. Didn't I know there were three sides to every story, your side, my side, and the truth?

An old Fall River lawyer was contacted, one who'd once represented my uncle. The lawyer in turn wrote me an elegant letter saying that Uncle Horace was a well-regarded philanthropist who gave away thousands of dollars to charity, and

---

2   For some reason, this was my father's favorite line of anything I've ever written. Before he died he'd call and say, "Let me talk to Turkeyboy."

3   This is neither here nor there, either, but now I'm told my career will take off when I write a viral essay. Suddenly, I'm fond of footnotes.

that he most certainly did not recognize the appalling cari-
cature in the story.

I loved my uncle. He smoked a pipe and sputtered when
he spoke. Even when he was destitute and living in the back
of his mother's little house on Woodlawn Street, he still
lectured anybody who'd come near him about the threat
of creeping socialism. He once told me he'd lunched with
Chiang Kai-shek.

"Friendly guy," he said. "Small hands."

I mourn him, like I mourn my grandparents and all my
Fall River relatives. They've all vanished and left me here to
remember them in silence. They were a loud, cackling people.
As a kid, coming out to Fall River from the simmering doom
of my father's house in Chicago was to enter a wondrous land
where people laughed, ate too much, snored thunderously.
Both my grandparents snored like beached, happy walruses.
Until Fred died and left Sally alone for thirty years.

Games. Of course I'm playing games. It's never brought
their laughter, their snores. And the seventy-five-dollar check
the *Chronicle* sent me? That's been spent.

Another true story my grandmother told me: In the year
before he died, my grandfather used what little he had left,
the little that Horace hadn't managed to steal from him, to
help pay for Horace's legal bills. They were brothers-in-law,
for god's sake. Horace was married to my grandmother's favorite sister, Josephine. My grandmother would have murdered him if he didn't pony up when Horace and Josephine
needed it most.

And this, too, HBO, is also true. I've got my grandfather's
financial records, all his account books, including the last
one with the red line across the page, as well as a contemporaneous article from the *Fall River Herald*, detailing the

bankruptcy proceedings, which includes an account of the creditor meeting where Horace's remaining assets were doled out to the big fish, leaving smaller creditors (i.e., relatives) in the lurch. And I know, because yes, my grandmother Sarah (Sally) Kaplan told me, that there was an estate sale where all Uncle Horace's and Josephine's belongings were laid out on the lawn in front of their beautiful house on Highland Avenue in Fall River. The Tiffany lamps, Chippendale chairs, Chinese lamps, Turkish vases, Pakistani rugs—those two traveled everywhere—were all sold off cheap, one by one by one. And my grandmother, that liar, wept as she stuffed a few dollars raised on behalf of her sister into her blouse.

Noon

» 42 «

DRUNK AS A GOOSE ON A CONVULSING AMERICAN EAGLE flight (operated by Air Wisconsin) heading home to Chicago. The pilot calls this moderate chop. In an attempt to settle my nerves, I'm reading Isaac Babel's "Guy de Maupassant"— Babel's irreverent homage to his irreverent hero.

St. Petersburg, the winter of 1916, and the narrator, a Jew with a fake passport and not a kopeck to his name, is hired to help translate a new edition of Maupassant's short stories. We just thumped into something solid. An armored cloud? The dawn of the Russian Revolution might not be the best moment to bring out a translation of short stories by a syphilitic Frenchman, but story writers or their translators aren't known for their timing. Can I get another bottle of this warm white wine? I can't. The flight attendants have double-strapped themselves into their jump seats, their expressions steely, unreadable—

American Eagle operated by Air Wisconsin. What does that even mean?

There's a reason the arms dealer, Bendersky, is throwing money away on Maupassant. His wife, the voluptuous Raisa, is the translator. When the broke Jew arrives at the mansion wearing a borrowed dinner jacket, the first thing Raisa gushes is:

"Maupassant is the only passion of my life."

The fact that she's a god-awful translator only makes her line more magnificent. Raisa's translations are wearisome, uninspired, too correct; they're stiff, flat nothings. How is it that a person—isn't this true of most of us?—can spend a lifetime loving something and still have zero idea how it came to be or how to replicate it? This zattling piece of multimillion-dollar junk. An overhead bin just opened and a duffel bag fell on a woman who laughed. She laughed. And the narrator takes Raisa's translations home with him, revises them, makes them sing. Sing as a Maupassant story must sing, with such a simple, easeful melody that you never see the jab coming until it's already between your eyes.

For the past ten minutes I've been sitting here alone in my little cone of personal light. My seatmate, a man in a tracksuit, is leaning toward me, his chin inches from my shoulder. He's snoring gentle, oblivious, trusting little snores as we bumble over Buffalo. I want to whisper, hot breath in his meaty ear, *Listen, Maupassant is the only passion of my life.*

After days of work, the narrator and Raisa translate "The Confession." In this story, Polyte, a carriage driver, says to Celeste, a young redheaded girl who's taking her cream, eggs, and chickens to sell at the market in town, "But when are we going to have our bit of fun, *ma belle*?" Celeste rebuffs him: "What's your meaning, Monsieur Polyte?"

It takes two years of trips back and forth to town, but

Monsieur Polyte does, eventually, enjoy his bit of fun. Maupassant's jab: Celeste is pregnant and desperately needs the money. She can no longer afford the rides into town. Babel's narrator, though, toys with the story, seems to pretend she wasn't forced into it:

> The white nag, its mouth pink with age, went
> slowly. The merry sunlight of France surrounded
> the large coach that was shut off from the world
> by a rusty hood. A lad and a girl need no music ...

The merry sunlight of France? A lad and a girl need no music? Right. All that's required is a character to be broke and desperate. It's twisted stuff, but the translator and translator's helper can't help but be aroused. *You're a funny one, Raisa growls.* And the two of them have their bit of fun, too. If anybody can wrench ecstasy out of darkness, it's Isaac Babel. It's like dancing on someone's grave. But don't we? Aren't we constantly, every day, dancing on graves? The narrator bumps into the bookshelf and all twenty-nine volumes of Maupassant crash to the carpet. Youth and hunger, genius and passion. Lust and compulsion. Manipulation and insanity. My seatmate's drool gleams in the light, a delicate thread, stretching from his lower lip to my shoulder. Only connect. Meantime, Bendersky, the arms dealer, is still at the opera. He'll be gone for hours. Fly on, Air Wisconsin.

Later—ambling home, the narrator of "Guy de Maupassant" says:

> I was sober and could have walked on a single
> board, but it was much better to stagger, and I

swayed from side to side, singing loudly in a language I had only just invented.

Remember? When you were sober and you staggered anyway?

» 43 «

Jews lived in Markley. Who knows how these things start? It wasn't as if the university sent out a bulletin: *Pssst, the Jew dorm is Markley.* And yet, somehow, we knew. The information passed on through generations of students. An oblong box half a mile long, uniform urine-yellow walls, door after door after door. Warehouse of beds. Mausoleum of hormones. Twelve hundred eighteen-year-olds packed tight. Reek of sweat and body odor. As if the building itself were made not of brick and cement and plaster but of secretions that had glommed, caked.

I was only dimly aware that somewhere beyond the dorm was, allegedly, a significant university, but what did libraries, laboratories, concerts, lectures, galleries, museums have on sorority pledges from Bloomfield Hills, Shaker Heights, Ladue? A ludicrous phrase, losing your virginity, unless you focus on the loss part, it being one loss among many others. Felicity Stein was tall with short black hair and, like me, an English major. She was funny; she was sarcastic. She said I was all right, for the moment, anyway. *It's only second semester freshman year.* Did she say this or is it just the look on her face that I'm remembering? We'd been hanging out with each other for a couple of weeks and were now parked on my futon pretending to study (I was pretending) for a midterm on the Modernists. In a poem, I stumbled over the word *knew*. Felicity said it was a double entendre.

"I don't get it."

"In the biblical sense. You know, Adam and Eve getting to know each other?"

"I wouldn't know."

"What do you mean?"

"I mean I lied about it all through senior year of high school."

"Honestly?"

I was like a blind rat in some experiment. Felicity in her ΣΔT sweatpants.

I panted, "Honestly."

"Where's the roommate?"

"He's in the hospital. An infection, it's pretty bad. They're keeping him for observation."

"Lock the door."

I locked the door and shoved a chair under the knob. We fell back on the futon. Felicity gripped my neck with both hands and said, "Who are you racing?"

"Mankind."

My roommate was the nicest guy, Kenneth from Cheboygan. (He happened not to be Jewish. I imagine he didn't fill out the preference form and someone in the housing office thought, *Well, here's an interesting opportunity for social engineering, plunk him with the out-of-state Jews.*) When he came home maybe eight minutes later, Kenneth unlocked the door but it wouldn't give and so he pushed against it until the chair gave way. He flipped on the light. There we were in the buttery fluorescence. Instead of coming apart, Felicity and I locked even closer and clung together, motionless.

"Ken, thank god, you're all right!"

"Huh?"

Now I try to see the moment from Kenneth's point of view. He'd come to college to study, to become educated. He had a timer on his desk. When he sat down to read, he'd set it for two hours. He was too polite to ever say it but he must have thought my friends and I were uncouth primates with our parents' credit cards.

Kenneth stood there and stared at his corduroy reading pillow. I'd borrowed it to class up the futon a little. He stared at the pillow as if its misuse were the violation, not the fact that I'd locked him out of his own room on a Tuesday night during midterms. Felicity and I tried to cover up by wrapping ourselves in a tumble of stray clothes and blankets.

I think he put the image of us out of his mind almost immediately. I don't remember his ever mentioning what happened the whole rest of freshman year. But at that moment he said, "So, what's up, man?"

"Not much, man, how about you?"

Kenneth left for the communal bathroom to brush his teeth. Felicity started rooting around for her sweatpants. "Let us go then, you and I," I said.

"Let's don't," she said. "Let's never."

I hear from her sometimes. She's a clinical psychologist, three kids. She lives outside Philadelphia.

» 44 «

I'LL BE DOING SOMETHING, ANYTHING, THE DISHES, AND I'll look out the window at the road, the carless, quiet road, and I'll see myself falling—from where? Nowhere, just falling—or worse, infinitely worse, my daughter or my son falling, falling—and I'll be reminded again of Rita Dove's zeppelin rising and the three men, the one who jumps off early and lands safely, the one who hangs on, and the other one, the third man, who, as the airship *Akron* rises higher, higher, loses his grip and lets go. Dove describes him as clawing the air as he drops. To claw you need something tangible to dig your fingers into. Dirt, someone's face. To claw at the air like that when there's nothing, not a thing in the world . . .

> muscles and adrenaline
> failing and fell

In the next stanza, a fourth man, Thomas, who witnessed the *Akron* floating out of control—and notice that it *floated* out of control, giving a sense of how slow-motion this all must have seemed at the time—is standing in a vacant lot, that night, thinking about what he's seen.

> Here I am intact
> and faint-hearted.

It's the image of the third man clawing the air but also this, a different man, Thomas, standing in the stillness, reflecting on what he'd seen. You'd think he was safe. How wrong. How wrong because even while standing in an empty, earthbound lot there's no protection from visions. Haven't you felt this? The need to brace yourself in a quiet, windless moment? Nothing around that might hurt you or anybody you love, and still?

We're all faint-hearted until it's you or me who tries to claw the air as the dumb blimp rises. I'm not saying it's tougher to be the witness, I'm only trying to say that the notion of our being intact in the stillness is ultimately an illusion, a nothingness we cling to, like the third man clings, muscles and adrenaline failing.

» 45 «

THE INHERENT FAILURE OF PHOTOGRAPHS TO PROVIDE consolation for the loss of the person in the picture. That's Yoel Hoffmann, an Israeli born in Romania. A Jew and a Buddhist. In addition to his novels—and to call them novels is to honor the word *novel*—he also translated, from the Japanese, *The Sound of the One Hand: 281 Koans with Answers.*

Somewhere I have a picture of Sam taken at Half Moon Lake, Michigan. Every once in a while, I come across it in a drawer among stray papers. A gusty day and Sam's long hair is rising over her shoulders in a swirl. She's squinting because she's looking directly into the sun. She's wearing a white shirt with big buttons and cutoff shorts. Is she holding a flower? I can't find the picture. I only find it when I'm not looking for it. I think she's holding a flower. She's leaning against the front bumper of my aunt Gert's Buick Century. Aunt Gert wasn't my aunt. She was my stepfather's aunt. The car was parked in Aunt Gert's driveway when she died. Dan said, Take it. Gert won't notice. Sam's hair wild in the wind. Was she holding a dandelion? No, bigger. A sunflower? Her eyes are as blue as my dead father's. You can't see Half Moon Lake because the car's blocking it but that's where we were. Did we swim? She's not dressed to swim but that wouldn't have stopped Sam. She'd have ditched the shirt and cutoffs and jumped in. I can't remember. Maybe it was too cold. Later, we drove my dead aunt's car back to Ann Arbor and immediately, upon reaching her place on East University, ran upstairs to her room and fucked like rabbits because Sam's roommate would be home any minute. Sam would not approve of this recollection for a number of reasons. But at a certain point don't the assorted scraps of our lives enter the public domain? Forgotten Ann Arbor days, shouldn't they be part of some permanent record?

Hoffmann. A specialist in joyous sorrow. He makes the most basic truths read like he's divulging secrets. To read Hoffmann is to have an intimate conversation with an elusive friend, one you only ever run into by chance. When you see this friend, he leans in close and whispers something mysterious, mundane, essential:

For what is a man if not Uncle Shamu.

Without another word, he vanishes, coat flapping, around a corner. There's a weightlessness in Hoffmann's prose that's contradictory. He makes me feel alive, buoyant, and, at the same time, I'm all the more conscious of the plodding gravity of everything I remember. Take this sentence from *The Book of Joseph*, a Holocaust book that doesn't mention the Holocaust because the people in it are only trying to live their lives and have no sense (who would?) that they are part of any history being written in stone.

As the years went by Chaya-Leah's face receded, and when Joseph tries to recall her appearance he can see her only through a cloud of fog.

Toward the end of *The Book of Joseph*, the prose breaks into poetry because there's no other way to say what Hoffmann is trying to say about all that will be lost, every mundane, forgettable moment:

An empty cognac bottle in the synagogue yard.
Someone comes out from under the bridge
and yawns . . .

Sam would say emphatically that we never fucked like rabbits. And she'd say her roommate couldn't have cared less what we did behind closed doors. Sam's version is the more correct. I also now remember that before we went upstairs that day, she played a Taj Mahal record that had belonged to her father. We listened to "Take a Giant Step." Sam danced, I watched her dance, slowly, by herself, in that way she tried to teach me once. *Don't move your feet so much; the music, if it's in you at all, it's in your shoulders.* Sam danced with her shoulders. I watched. The two of us, the music, Sam's shoulders rising and falling. I'm sitting here at the kitchen table. The dog's in the corner, moaning in her sleep. Thirty years. How can something so alive be so gone? How many ways to ask this? Then we did, we went up the creaky steps of that yellow brick rental on East University to Sam's room. By that point we were so exhausted from the long day in the sun and the long drive that we fucked like tired horses.

» 46 «

IN THE OPENING PAGES OF BETTE HOWLAND'S MEMOIR, *W-3*, she describes the aftermath of swallowing a bottle of pills. She writes: "I pretty quickly regretted what I'd done . . ." She didn't become frantic. She called her doctor and left a message with his answering service.

Pause here and think about it. You feel the regret right away, but you also know that soon you're going to be even more tired than you already feel. For years, you've been nothing but tired. Is there any easier surrender? When the doctor called back and received no answer, he called an ambulance. I'm trying to remain in the in-between, in the before, when she was still awake. It had been on her mind for some time, she writes. She had troubles with men, troubles with money. Howland was raising two boys by herself in Chicago. And yet: so soon after, regret. As if both the act and regret were lying in wait for her and now would compete with each other, the act having the distinct advantage. Regret like a silent passenger had been there all along. How feeble compared with the mighty indifference of that impending sleep.

> Evidently I had gotten undressed, a creature of habit, and lain down between the sheets in an orderly fashion. I never heard the telephone.

The only thing separating these two sentences is the slender thread of one woman's breathing. "I have never remembered," she writes, "it was just as if no one was home."

After being treated in the emergency room, Howland was placed in the locked psychiatric ward of a South Side hospital, a place where she met a swath of Chicagoans, from professors to junkies, housewives to mechanics, heiresses to hairdressers, florists to pimps. Maybe a psych ward is the one place you could possibly meet people from every corner of any city.

There's a scene with Howland and a psychiatrist. It starts with a sense of hope. "That was what we were in the hospital for," she says. To have therapeutic conversations with doctors. That's how you got cured.

> "Now how about sex?" asks Dr. Doremy, clasping the edge of his steel desk and rolling himself up to it. His swivel chair keeps sliding away every time he crosses his long legs. "What is its importance to you in a relationship?"
>
> I say it's really very important; but then again, it isn't everything . . .
>
> "Okay good." Folding his arms across his narrow chest. "You understand about that then."

Lately, I've begun to read in my sleep. I'll drop off in the middle of a sentence and I'll keep going. I don't mean I fall asleep reading. I mean I keep reading after I fall asleep. Ghost sentences. It's here, during Howland's conversation, where I nodded off, filling in what happened next myself, sentences I can't quote here because they made sense only in my unconscious. This is starting to sound mystical. It's just something that happened. The cadence of Howland's prose—so direct, it's knifelike—leaked into my brain and, head slumped, eyes closed, the scene carried on. I listened to Howland and the doctor talk past each other until the session was over.

Group meetings in the morning, group meetings in the afternoon. Sometimes, the patients took a field trip and went bowling. Howland nearly completely disappears into the stories of the people she now lives among. This is how she endures it. She becomes, first and foremost, a witness. There's Fran, Cootie, Simone, Zelma, Charlotte, Davy Jones, Elke, Basil, Guz, Jesse, Deronda, Henry, Trudy, Georgia, La Donna, Yvette . . . Newcomers to W-3 always protested that they didn't belong there. *Me? Here with these loons?* Yet how quickly a patient, any patient, no matter how troubled, burdened, wounded, or yes, out of their head, falls into line, into the schedule. The sleepless nights, the monotonous days.

Some afternoons, Howland's two boys would wave up to her from the parking lot.

» 47 «

I'M STANDING UNDER THE EL TRACKS ON NOYES STREET in Evanston. This would be the spring of 1990. I look up at the light piercing through the wooden slats. A train has just passed and there's a stillness and the light is poking through. I stop and stand in that patch of darkness on the otherwise sunny street. Ian, my roommate, the night before, swallowed twelve Benadryl tabs. After lying down on his bed for a while he managed to hold off sleep and stagger to the health clinic on campus. He didn't make it all the way. He collapsed on the sidewalk outside the clinic. A security guard found him lying in the flowers.

His girlfriend, Lizzy, told me all of it that night at two in the morning. She'd come to pick up some of Ian's clothes. She kept saying she should be crying. "Why aren't I crying?" I hardly knew her. I hardly knew Ian. I hardly knew anybody. I was a transfer student. Lizzy ended up sleeping in my bed because she didn't want to sleep in his. I slept on the couch. It smelled of old beer, which smells like urine. I woke up late. Lizzy was gone. I'd missed my classes. I got dressed and went out, not intending to go anywhere in particular. That's when I walked down Noyes and stopped under the tracks.

What am I getting at?

Only that I have this recurring vision of standing there and staring up into the light leaking through the slats. The silence of a train having just passed, the absence formed by that clatter. I thought of Ian, lurching forward, trying to outrace those pills. I wondered if, to pull off something heroic, you had to first do something senseless.

I'd answered an ad pinned to a bulletin board in the student center. *Room available, Decently Cheap.* Ian was an English major also, though he never went to class. He said he wouldn't read an assigned book if it was the last book on earth. He wrote stories in a spiral notebook that he never showed anybody. He said the way to become a writer was to take a story and copy it word for word in your own hand, tricking yourself into believing that you, too, could write "The Fall of the House of Usher." See? Your hand just did. Every once in a while I try to find him. There doesn't seem to be any trace of Ian. Wherever he is, alive or dead, he seems to have found a way to be invisible. It was good advice about copying by hand. I still do it. You can trick yourself into believing a lot of things.

» 48 «

IN GORDON BOWKER'S BIOGRAPHY OF JAMES JOYCE, I learn that Joyce accompanied his twenty-six-year-old daughter, Lucia, to her first appointment with Carl Jung. This was in Zurich in 1933. Jung described Joyce as having enlarged pupils suggesting the "full-eyed concentration of a wild animal." It seems Jung was more focused on the writer than the patient. For his part, Joyce wasn't wowed by the psychoanalyst. He once called Jung the Swiss Tweedle Dum, not to be confused with the Viennese Tweedle Dee. So desperate to help his daughter, he'd try anything.

Twenty years later, Jung would write that in his opinion Joyce was a kind of schizophrenic by choice while Lucia was the real deal. At the time, after a month, Jung said to Joyce only that he simply wasn't sure of the best course of action in Lucia's case. Psychoanalysis might help. Then again, it might not. Who knows? The human shadow speaks with a thousand voices.

Though *Ulysses* put him to sleep (twice) and he said that it would mean the same thing if read backward, Jung was nonetheless convinced that Joyce was a prophet, "an unwitting mouthpiece of the secrets of his time." The bill for Lucia's treatment was 3,600 francs. It should have been more. Jung gave Joyce the prophet discount.

For a few months, she was calmer. She began taking long

car trips and playing billiards. Lucia told her father that what she really wanted was a quiet garden and a dog. Then she set her room on fire again. A day later she blacked her face with ink. They put her in restraints. They locked her in a room with bars. Joyce's friends urged him to have her committed formally. He refused and took her with him to Paris. From there she traveled alone to Ireland (her father had no interest, he was through with Ireland), believing that a return to the homeland where she'd once been happy as a young girl might . . . but Ireland was not what she expected or remembered.

Is anywhere?

In her lucid moments, and there were a great many, Lucia once asked a doctor if there was any cure for her short of murder. She sent telegrams to dead friends. Joyce took her from doctor to doctor, from clinic to clinic. One physician in Zurich had diagnosed her as having a curable blood disorder, and Joyce clung to this for years. I don't want to know who died first.

» 49 «

EARLY IN *ULYSSES*, LEOPOLD BLOOM REMEMBERS THE midwife, Mrs. Thornton in Denzille Street, a jolly old woman: *She knew from the first poor little Rudy wouldn't live.* She was right. The boy lasted eleven days. Had he lived longer, would his father have become such a wanderer?

Every once in a while, deep in a crowded paragraph: Rudy.

See him grow up. Hear his voice in the house.

In chapter 15, after leaving Bella Cohen's brothel, Bloom sees, or thinks he sees, the grown-up boy himself, eleven years old now, dressed in a suit and wearing glass shoes— what are glass shoes?—leaning against a wall, holding a book in his hand. He's reading from right to left, like my mother's cousin Solly, who everybody called "our yeshiva bocher" because he'd once (for three weeks) studied to be a rabbi. Rudy's a vision? A hallucination? Aren't these as much of our experience as our own flesh and blood? My kids sleeping, visions of my kids sleeping . . .

Certain Joyce scholars say that Rudy's premature death is the cause of Bloom's impotence. (As well as, they say, the catalyst for his symbolic return to Judaism.) Joyce delighted in screwing with the professors. He knew they'd be chasing their tails till the end of time. To turn Rudy into a representation of sexual dysfunction is the worst kind of academic idiocy—as if the loss of a child has to mean anything more than the loss of a child.

Bloom, dizzy and zonked from the battering at Bella Cohen's, shouts inaudibly to his son. *Rudy!*

Why inaudibly? Aren't our most pleading shouts the ones we don't shout out loud? The ones that stay bottled in our throats?

Rudy!

And the kid—this dead kid—looks into his father's eyes without seeing anybody and goes on reading.

» 50 «

FLORIDA, SANIBEL ISLAND. WE WERE IN THE KITCHEN OF some condo. I was a senior in college and down there on vacation to see my father and his girlfriend and my father started in again about what a cunt my mother was and I went after him with a kitchen knife. My father had been slicing cantaloupe and the knife was lying there on the counter a little wet from the cantaloupe juice and so help me god I'm going to plunge it into my father's chest and he for his part stands there and waits for me to do it, proud that at last I'm demonstrating the possession of a few of the balls I must have inherited from him, and meanwhile his girlfriend shrieks, *Police! Somebody! Anybody! Neighbor!* but my father holds up his hand, no, no, wait, let's see how this scene plays out.

51

YOU GET TO THE POINT WHERE ELEGIES FEEL FRAUDU-
lent. A self-involved too-late gasp of appreciation. James
Alan McPherson. He's been dead how long now?

Once, during class, he played an old cassette tape of an interview he'd conducted with Richard Pryor back in the '70s.
Mostly it consisted of Pryor laughing so hard he gasped for
breath. Imagine a man who could make Richard Pryor laugh.
There were a few pauses when you could clearly hear Pryor
snorting coke. Then Pryor would go back to laughing at something that McPherson had muttered under his breath. Why
did he play us this tape? It wasn't to boast he'd hung out with a
celebrity. That would have been the last thing he'd have cared
about. It was about two people talking, laughing, all guards
down, open-souled. That's what he'd wanted us to hear.

We were grad students. Full of ourselves, our youth, our
talent; we were only waylaid in Iowa City for a couple of years
to fatten up our genius. McPherson didn't knock us for being
such dipshits. He knew that a certain amount of dipshittery
went along with being a grad student.

He liked to collect examples of people being sponta-
neously generous. A neo-Nazi is pelted by a rock at a rally in
Skokie. The Nazi, a pimpled kid, falls in the street bleeding.
A protester rushes to him, kneels, holds his bleeding head,
protects him with her body. A McPherson moment. When a

humane instinct overcomes the script. Not a photo op he was after. And he'd have preferred it not be celebrated as anything other than an ordinary thing to do. A kid's hurt (stupid kid, misguided kid, evil kid); still, she comforts him, shields him.

In 1996, I permanently borrowed a first edition of McPherson's *Hue and Cry* from the Coralville Public Library in Iowa. I did so for three reasons. (1) The book hadn't been checked out in years and therefore I decided that the people of Coralville had lost the right to it. (2) *Hue and Cry*, at that time, as a result of an obscure publishing feud, was incredibly hard to find. (3) The book contained the story "Gold Coast," arguably McPherson's most enduring example of his infinitely open heart.

McPherson wouldn't have approved. Had I confessed, he'd have rummaged his house for a precious copy and given it to me immediately, and yet he might have appreciated the human contradiction of my simultaneously celebrating a book's expansive benevolence while hoarding it for myself.

If I had any talent for memorizing, which I don't, I'd like to learn "Gold Coast" by heart so I could recite it to myself in bookless moments like a prayer. It's the story of a friendship between an old Irish janitor and a young writer, and opens with this line:

> That spring when I had a great deal of potential
> and no money at all, I took a job as a janitor.

Sullivan, the head janitor, teaches Rob, the apprentice, the ropes. He gives him the lowdown on who's who in the building. Which apartments have Jews. There are more Jews here than anybody, Sullivan says. He tells Rob about the old ladies who will try, against house rules, to leave cat litter out for the janitor. The rules specifically state that people have to take the cat litter out themselves. "You tell them to put it in a bag and take it out themselves." Sullivan didn't really hate Jews or spinsters, Rob explains, "He was just bitter toward anyone better off than himself." Sullivan's wife has been going insane for years. She can only walk as far as the front steps of the building, where she sits, daily, wearing a blue hat and muttering to nobody. Sullivan's wife loves only her dog. And Sullivan himself is stone lonely. He just needs someone to talk to. He calls Rob at all hours of the night, asks him to come down to the boiler room for a quick drink.

Rob's in love. He's got a girl who happens to be white, just as he happens to black, and though people are constantly reminding them of this difference, the two of them are, for the moment, happy together. Rob's writing is going well. He's got better things to do than listen to the old janitor jabber on. Still, he meets Sullivan in the boiler room.

"My Meg's not in the best of health, you know," he would say, handing the bottle to me.
"She's just old."
"The doctors say she should be in an institution."
"That's no place to be."
"I'm sick myself, Rob. I can't take much more. She's crazy."
"Anybody who loves animals can't be crazy."

Who's got time for this? Rob's got love to make, a book to write. All his potential to be realized. And still Jimmy Sullivan talks. He tells Rob how he once sat at a bar next to James

Michael Curley himself, the supremest crook ever to grace the mayorship of Boston. Memories of a lifetime and Rob knows that they are being sold cheap. Sullivan only wants somebody to listen to him. Sullivan talks and he talks. He talks about Medicare, beatniks, civil rights.

> Then I would start to edge toward the door, and he would see that he could hold me no longer, not even by declaring that he wanted to be an honorary Negro because he loved the race so much.

You know this moment? When your need to talk is so overwhelming you'll say anything at all to hold your audience? Maybe the stories that most ache come out of this impulse. We're desperate to tell them before it's too late, even if it's only into the ear of somebody who's hardly listening anymore, who's got someplace he'd rather be. Maybe something we say will stick, be remembered. Rob eventually leaves the job, the building, but this doesn't mean he's ever able to leave Sullivan behind. The image, at the end, of Jimmy Sullivan and his wife trudging through Harvard Square carrying those heavy grocery bags, I'll never shake it.

52

A DUMB-LUCK, WINDFALL ROMAN YEAR, AND SOME nights I'd wander across Monteverde toward the Vatican, past the Garibaldi statue, past the parking lot with the sleeping tour buses, and climb a hill overlooking St. Peter's. A road dead-ended at the top. It was said to be a place prostitutes took clients. Other couples frequented the top of that hill, too. Roman apartments are small and many people live with their parents. I'd stand under the trees and watch the cars bounce happily in the dark and think about Garibaldi— not the general, the pharmacist. He owned the drugstore uptown. Once I stole a Kit Kat. It wasn't the first time, only the first time I'd been caught, and Mr. Garibaldi shot out from behind the counter like a fat cheetah and nearly caught the banana seat of my five-speed as I absconded. He stood in the middle of Central Avenue bellowing at the top of his lungs, "Halt, thief!" Sergeant Kraus, planted on his motorcycle and gnawing a sandwich after an arduous morning of chalking tires and issuing parking tickets, said, "Let the kid go, Cesare. I'm still on lunch."

Later that year, after my brother got a job delivering prescriptions, Mr. Garibaldi took the cost of the Kit Kat out of his first paycheck, saying, You are thy brother's keeper. It didn't bother my brother. On that job, he stole a lot more than Kit Kats. All the pills he pocketed fetched a good price at the high school. That's not true. My brother didn't deal drugs. He gave away drugs.

In the dark, amid the trees, I watched the Fiats bounce.

In Robert Lowell's "Skunk Hour," he wrote:

> One dark night,
> my Tudor Ford climbed the hill's skull;
> I watched for love-cars . . .

And a few lines down:

> I myself am hell;
> nobody's here—

Makes sense. We carry it around. Hell's portable. Other people's love-cars only make it worse.

Garibaldi, the pharmacist, was built like a tank, but yes, he could move like a big cat. A few years before he died, he sold his inventory to the Walgreens on Route 41 and retired up to Lake Geneva, Wisconsin. At first people were upset but Walgreens had better prices. Before that, though, whenever I'd go to Garibaldi's, he'd pinch his eyes and stalk every move I made. And why shouldn't he have? He had a livelihood to protect. I get it. I'm the same way now. God knows I'll defend my little kingdom with all the strength I've got. Still, there are those nights I lurk in the trees and watch.

» **53** «

In *To Float in the Space Between*, a meditation on the poet Etheridge Knight, Terrance Hayes writes that a poem might be understood as a kind of house. Basic notions of order, Hayes says, tend to insist that we find, in this house, certain pieces of furniture in the expected places. Beds in the bedroom, shower in the bathroom, TV in the family room . . . *But how wonderful to find a use for a couch in the kitchen . . . how wonderful to find your mother reclining on the couch while she stirs something delicious.*

If a poem is a house, praise dissonance, let there be a couch in the kitchen.

That year Naomi and I lived in Cincinnati. We lived in a run-down Queen Anne. Our back window looked out upon an overgrown yard that bordered an alley. We were close enough to the zoo that we'd hear the elephants trumpet for dinner. And a big shaggy couch was stranded in our kitchen. We were able to ram the thing through the back door but we hadn't thought of the fact that the hallway connecting the kitchen to the front room was L-shaped. We were nearly happy that year in Ohio. Until a moment ago, I'd forgotten all about the couch.

Nobody stirred anything delicious in the kitchen. We never cooked much. Most nights we went up the block to Biaggio's, the little Italian place on Ludlow. Biaggio, an effusive man who reminded us of Pavarotti, made an excellent soup. Little pellets of meat shaped like goat turds bobbed up and down in sweet broth. I've conjured this soup in my dreams.

Biaggio would say, "You two again? Can't either of you cook? Your mothers taught you nothing? What about a chicken pot pie? Boil a couple of hot dogs?"

During the day Naomi worked on her applications to film school. Monday, Wednesday, and Friday, I drove up to Oxford to teach composition at Miami of Ohio. Naomi had a job at a community television station. One of the shows she produced featured a woman reciting Bible verses while doing aerobics. That was also the year, this was in 2000, the Cincinnati police shot an eighth unarmed Black man in a row. There were protests in Over-the-Rhine. Fires. A curfew. Naomi went down to film at the police station and almost got trampled by a cop on a horse.

To Float in the Space Between is subtitled: *A Life and Work in Conversation with the Life and Work of Etheridge Knight.* Hayes expressly says that the book isn't a biography of Knight, who died in 1991. Knight wrote, among other seminal American poems, "The Idea of Ancestry." The third stanza goes like this:

> I have the same name as 1 grandfather, 3 cousins,
>   3 nephews,
> and 1 uncle. The uncle disappeared when he was
>   15, just took
> off and caught a freight (they say). He's discussed
>   each year

when the family has a reunion, he causes
uneasiness in
the clan, he is an empty space.

We've all got someone who's caught a freight, or a bus
or a flight. Or just drove away. Or who divorced you or you
divorced them. People as empty spaces.

No, this is not a biography of Etheridge Knight, Terrance
Hayes says. It's part homage, part reckoning, part collection
of stray, intimate details. Hayes calls it notes for a future
biographer, but his method seems to me the only honest way
of trying to construct an actual life on the page. A gathering
of fragments. Of the stories that get told about us. Of the stories we told. Unordered, like our thoughts on any given day
we lived. Hayes:

> *Yusef's stories about Etheridge were full of gaps
> and silences.*

Sometimes, on weekend afternoons, Naomi would fall asleep
on the couch in the kitchen with her bare feet hanging over
the side. 3424 Brookline Avenue, Cincinnati. After Cincinnati we went to California, where everything eventually went
to hell. Because doesn't everything go to hell in California?

» 54 «

A YOUNG GIRL RAISED ON A FARM IN THE FARTHEST reaches of northeastern California, up near the Oregon and Nevada borders, leaves home at sixteen. She makes her way to San Francisco. It's the middle 1930s. On Market Street sidewalk shouters are preaching the virtues of the New Deal. The girl, Rose, finds a room in a boardinghouse in a run-down neighborhood. She aspires to write and falls in with a group of writers and artists. To make ends meet, she finds a job at an insurance company.

Ella Leffland's *Mrs. Munck*. It came out in 1970. I believe it was her first book. She's in her nineties now, and has pub-lished many other books, including a seven-hundred-page novel about Hitler's deputy, Hermann Göring. They made a movie of *Mrs. Munck*, a comedy, apparently, with Diane Ladd and Bruce Dern. The novel isn't a comedy.

Rose sleeps with her boss at the insurance company. Out of inertia, she continues to see him. Rose is poor. Mr. Leary is rich and married. He keeps coming to her room. Rose gets pregnant. Leary promptly fires her. After the baby, Gloria, is born, Leary refuses to recognize or support the child in any way. Rose is tenacious and attempts to bring a paternity suit. Leary returns to her room and demands she knock it off. It's winter, cold. The baby is crawling around on the floor. Rose throws something heavy, I forget what, at Leary's head. She misses. A gas heater topples over and falls on the baby. Rose tries to pull the gas burner off the child, but she can't; it's far too hot.

I left *Mrs. Munck* on a BART train years ago. I had maybe ten or fifteen pages left to go. I've never made any attempt to replace it. Leffland's depiction of Rose's numbness following the death of her daughter has remained lodged. The most desolate prose I'm sure I've ever read.

Of what comes after, I remember that months later, out of the fog of anguish and rage, a new Rose emerges. Years go by and Rose marries an acquaintance from the insurance company who happens to be Mr. Leary's nephew. The couple moves to a small house in what was then an underpopulated part of the East Bay, on the shore of the Carquinez Strait. This decades-long, loveless marriage is compressed into a few pages. Upon the death of her husband, Rose, now called Mrs. Munck, decides the time is now to take in a boarder.

Why—what about her late husband's elderly uncle, her old boss, Mr. Leary, who's now languishing away in a nursing home? He must hunger for family. And, after all, isn't Rose family?

The revenge in *Mrs. Munck* is as warped, methodical, and ruthless as it is justifiable. Leary, wheelchair-bound and terrified, wonders, each day he's in Rose's house, if she'll let him live out the next hour. Does she finally murder him? I don't know. Certain books, rare ones, you go on reading whether you are reading them or not. I'm still trapped, with Leary, in a little house overlooking the Carquinez Strait.

» 55 «

WE LEFT CALIFORNIA FOR A WHILE. WE RENTED A SMALL house in Tivoli, New York, a town up the highway from Bard College, where I was, nominally, teaching a class. A cartoonist lived a few doors down. He used to come by with his dog and the three of us would sometimes drink a few beers together on the front porch.

The previous year had been hell. Naomi's moods fishtailing all over. Mine, too. We rarely slept more than a few hours at a time. In the mornings we'd lie sprawled, the shades drawn, the light leaking, beaten to death by the night and our shouting at each other.

It wasn't any different in Tivoli. Did we think it would be? But, like I say, in the afternoons, the cartoonist would be walking his dog and he'd stop by our house and I'd grab beers and the three of us would sit on the porch and just shoot the shit. I don't know why I think so often about the cartoonist. We knew him only those few months. There was something about his kindness and lack of judgment. He carried a sketchbook with him and often showed us his drawings. He must have seen how starved we were for laughs. We'd become somebody's neighbors. Seemed so easy. All we had to do was live somewhere.

Also that fall, maybe as a result of the same optimism as the beers, the porch, the cartoonist and his dog, I went and got knee surgery for a torn meniscus. It wasn't remotely necessary, but it was the first time in a long time that I had decent health insurance. I'm not paying for it. I figured, why not a needless surgery? Strange the anesthesia. I remained awake for part of the operation. My leg like a fat piece of ham. I kept kneading it with my fingers and I could feel my skin but I couldn't feel myself feeling my skin. Or I felt my leg but it wasn't mine. It's hard to explain.

When I came to, I was alone. Naomi wasn't there. I'd driven myself to the hospital in the morning. The plan was that after the operation Naomi would take a cab to the hospital and drive us both back home in the car. I called her and there was no answer. A half hour later, I called again. I waited there in the bed in that hospital in Kingston. A nurse had to sign off that someone, a family member or a friend, had come in order for me to be permitted to leave. I waited a couple more hours, enjoying the drugs. I tried Naomi again, still no answer. Maybe if I'd had the cartoonist's number I'd have tried him. Instead, I called a cab. I dragged myself across the floor to the wheelchair that was parked in the corner of the room and gingerly rolled myself out of the hospital. Slow-motion escape. Nobody noticed. The cab brought me home. By then the drugs had worn off and I was trying not to scream bloody murder. The cabdriver helped me to the door.

In the kitchen, Naomi was making soup. She'd started to cook.

"Where were you?" I said.

"Where was I when?"

"After my operation."

"Oh, your operation. I made soup."

"I couldn't feel my leg. It was like I was paralyzed. Now I can feel it and it's—"

Naomi held out a spoon to my mouth. "Try some?"

"Let's get married," I said.

It was fall, she'd made soup.

My god, Vicodin. In bed floating. Like falling through clouds and clouds. Like my feet, my toes were stoned. A couple of nights into it, I was still floating but I couldn't sleep. I'd lie there and lie there. I managed to get out of bed and flounce down the steps. Somehow I made it out to the car. I craved motion and, since I couldn't walk, I figured I'd drive. I could have killed somebody, I could have killed myself. Maybe, loosely, that was the point, careening along the Taconic Parkway toward Hudson, a beautiful highway as highways go. Lots of trees. I couldn't see them but I knew they were out there in the dark, all that green.

» 56 «

EVERY FEW YEARS OR SO I GO TO VISIT MY DEAD AT BETH
El Cemetery in Fall River. It's across the street from a Cumber-
land Farms. My grandfather always said that being dead didn't
seem so bad if he could run over and grab a pack of cigarettes
and the *Fall River Herald*. On the brick post of the cemetery
gate there's an old bronze plaque that says, "Prepare thyself
in the vestibule that thou mayest enter the hall." I always stop
and read this and wonder how my preparations are going.
Because I live in Vermont now, I think of the vestibule as a
mudroom—crusty boots, raincoats, sweatshirts, dog leashes, a
twisted nest of extension cords, hats, a yoga mat, a mousetrap
with a petrified piece of cheese, the dog's water bowl, a broken
bike pump, old homework, lost socks, an uncapped tube of
sunblock, missing library books, a solo mitten.

Prepare thyself.

Among my dead is a lone grave, a little off to the side. *Murray Epstein 1941–1948*. Murray was my mother's cousin. He lived
in the apartment downstairs on Weetamoe Street with his parents, Aunt Doris and Uncle Irv. My mother lived upstairs with
her parents, my grandparents Sally and Fred Kaplan.

It's been told so many times. One morning, he cut himself,
on what is no longer remembered, and the bleeding wouldn't
stop. My mother, who was upstairs, remembers the screams.
It wasn't Murray. Aunt Doris was the one screaming, and

her screams alerted my grandfather, who, after warning my mother to stay put, bolted down the stairs.

My grandmother wasn't home at the time. It was a Saturday. She was out shopping. Later, she was the one who cleaned up the blood.

He was my great playmate, my mother always says, Murray was my little buddy.

But what was he like?

He was seven, I was nine, we ran around the house. What do you mean what was he like? He was a sweet kid with a temper. Once he poked me in the eye. He was the only brother I ever had.

It turned out the sweet kid had hemophilia. He was dead by the time they reached the hospital. Who knew? Isn't that what the tsars had? What's that got to do with my uncle Irv, a Jewish stationer?

The rumor, one that's been whispered among my relatives for nearly eighty years now, don't tell anybody, is that my mother and Murray's grandparents, my great-grandparents Molly and Max, were first cousins. Murray's hemophilia being prima facie evidence. Even closely held family secrets dissolve eventually into only words.

Doris and Irv kept a picture of Murray on top of the television. My mother says Aunt Doris never got over it. Sometimes in the middle of a conversation, to the end of her life, she'd turn away from whoever she was talking to, and wince.

How little time he had to prepare in the vestibule. I put a small rock beside the *M* in Murray's name to let him know I came by.

IF THE THINGS WE PUT IN PARENTHESES MIGHT BE DE-
scribed as the things we can't help but say (no matter how
much they distract), then I wonder if all sentences shouldn't
be in parentheses. From a moment in Tomas Tranströmer's
poem "Baltics," about his grandparents:

> (We're walking together. She's been dead for
> thirty years.)

What is it about prose, especially my own, that's begun
to feel so leaden? And what is it about a line of poetry that's
like the fleet bite of a mosquito? That imperceptible surgical
injection of the proboscis, in, out, finished—

> (We're walking together. She's been

My eyes, as so often happens, wander off. The grief that's
called to the surface by someone else's words. She used to
wait for me when I'd drive down to Fall River those years I
lived in Boston. I'd climb over the railing and come through
the sliding door without knocking. The sweet, pungent smell
of that little apartment, a kind of sugary rot, and she's rising
from the couch happy to see me but at the same time pissed
off at how late I am, again. *What, do you think I have nothing*

better to do than lounge around the house and wait all day for you? Do you know how many plans I canceled? How many of these shriekers and pouters I've had to put off so I could be available— And how these contradictory reactions didn't cancel each other out but instead merged into a begrudging relief that I'd made it down here alive, again. *Help yourself to the half sandwich in the fridge, it's tuna from Newport Creamery. Pretty good! And there are some of those shoestring potato chips you like.*

We didn't walk, we drove. All over Fall River. To the dressmakers, to the pharmacy, to the podiatrist. To the Chinese restaurant in the mall out by Airport Road. Even to the pool at her complex, which was just down the hill. We'd get in her little Plymouth Sundance and drive. At the pool was a social club. She wouldn't talk to her friends when I was with her. She could be haughty. I'd do laps in the little pool as best I could. She'd sit on the deck and read Anne Tyler. She said Anne Tyler can tell a story. When was I going to learn to tell a story?

> So you've met someone?
> What makes you say that?
> Clean shirt.
> It's that clean?
> Wishful looking!

She volunteered in the hospital gift shop, a job she liked. She liked to bring a little joy to people. I sell some chocolate, a stuffed animal. You'd think it wouldn't mean much. When it was time for me to leave her, she'd hand me my hat. Here's your hat, what's your hurry?

When I didn't have a hat she handed me one anyway. Here's your hat . . .

In March of her last year my mother brought her out to Chicago from Fall River. She was seventy-eight. (My mother went on paying the rent for her apartment as if this might hold her with us longer.) She died in Chicago, a foreign city, at Rush Presbyterian St. Luke's, in June 1995.

She had three sisters. Sally was the only one born in Massachusetts; the others, Ida, Frieda, and Josephine, were all born in Russia. Their mother died when Sally was seven and so Ida, Frieda, and Josephine raised her. Ida, Frieda, Josephine, and Sally all lived within a mile of one another their entire lives. Sally was always the motherless baby.

» **58** «

FOR WEEKS NOW I'VE BEEN CARRYING AROUND A BEATEN
green hardcover copy of Lorraine Hansberry's *The Sign in
Sidney Brustein's Window*. The play is about a thirty-five-
year-old Jewish bohemian in 1960s Greenwich Village. I wake
up every morning and think I'm still a thirty-five-year-old
Jewish bohemian. Thirty-five, long out of sight. In any case,
still bohemian in theory. Easy leftism, like being a Jew, runs
in the family. So maybe I can be forgiven for reading myself
into this play, throughout which Sidney Brustein struggles
from the opening scene to the last with marital complications, wavering political commitment, his overall place in
the universe . . . Sidney rants. He pontificates. He insults.
He charms. He drinks. At one point, he even falls asleep and
dozes, on stage, through a crucial scene.

It's not a short play. Critics complained at the time that
there was too much talking, which, given that it's a play, isn't
what a playwright wants to hear. Here's Sidney early on:

> Yes, I suppose I have lost the pretensions of the
> campus revolutionary, Alton. I do admit that I no
> longer have the energy, the purity, or the compre-
> hension to—"save the world." As a matter of fact,
> to get *real big* about it, I no longer even believe that
> spring must necessarily come at all. Or that if it

does, that it will bring forth anything more poetic
or insurgent than—the winter's dormant ulcers.

Winter's dormant ulcers? That's Sidney in full flourish.
I've come to love the pompous speechifier.

The other day, my car broke down in a small town called
Warren. As I waited for a tow I sat on the hood of my 2005
Subaru—oh, this neglected Outback—and read *The Sign
in Sidney Brustein's Window.* I love it when the car breaks
down. Take your time, AAA, I'm all good.

Warren, New Hampshire, is famous for one thing. They've
got a missile on the village green, which struck me as not irrelevant to the play I was reading. *Ideas, anybody, for what to
put on the green? Okay, a bandstand, that's one. A fountain,
all right, we'll put that on the list. Ball field? Okay! Decommis-
sioned nuclear warhead? Great, that's four good options. Shall
we take a vote?*

Lorraine Hansberry didn't fuck around. She once told off Bobby Kennedy to his face. Basically, she said if he was the best white America could muster, we were all in a hell of a lot of trouble. She didn't have it easy. She was a semi-closeted gay woman in the early '60s (out to her friends, not out to her public). In the last two years of her life, Hansberry suffered from debilitating pain on account of an initially undiagnosed cancer.

The Sign in Sidney Brustein's Window closed on Broadway the night of the morning she died, at thirty-four, in January 1965. The play wasn't a success, and now, aside from an occasional revival, it's largely forgotten. What happened, many wondered, to the young phenom who wrote *A Raisin in the Sun*? Her second play and there's only one Black character in it? And what is this? A satire of do-good white artists and intellectuals? Don't we already know they're full of shit?

True, Hansberry's critique of jibber-jabbering lefties is loud and clear. And yet Sidney and his wife, Iris, aren't bowling pins Hansberry sets up in order to knock down. They are a married couple who read like a married couple.

> **SIDNEY:** Where did you get the idea about these things to pass judgment on them?
> **IRIS:** From the same place you got the idea that you were an editor.

Another character, Mavis, Iris's sister, isn't subtly racist, she's an outspoken bigot. She's horrified that a third sister, Gloria, is considering marrying Alton, a Black Communist. (She can live, almost, with the commie part.) Even so, it's Mavis who delivers one of the fiercest lines of dialogue in the play:

I am standing here and thinking: how smug it is in bohemia. I was taught to believe that— creativity and great intelligence ought to make one expansive and understanding. That if ordinary people, among whom I have the sense to count myself, could not expect understanding from artists and—whatever it is that *you* are, Sidney—then where indeed might we look for it all?

Sidney himself can't help but admire Mavis a little after this shellacking. She's odious, but this doesn't mean Mavis isn't capable of genuine insight. Hansberry refuses, patently, to settle for stock characters lacking human complications.

For all the skewering of bourgeois poseurs, as I sat on my hood I found myself drawn to a different aspect of the play. It's a brief scene that begins Act Two. Sidney is lying on the stoop of the apartment with his banjo. It's dawn and he's entered what appears to be a trancelike state as he imagines himself up on some mountain where things are not only apolitical, they're pure.

> Presently **SIDNEY** picks up his banjo and, legs dangling over the patio, begins to pick it. The melody seems surely drawn from that other world which ever beckons him, a wistful, throbbing mountain blues.

Stage directions, those tiny unspoken stories within the story. At last, Sidney isn't simply a blabbering blowhard. He's picking a banjo, in early morning New York City. People, actual people, are never consistently themselves. Who knew Sidney Brustein played the banjo? Iris joins him on the stoop. What follows is a scene of tenderness. The pace slows down, the dialogue is less rapid-fire, and Hansberry allows these two damaged souls, this flailing couple, a possibility of connection that seemed so lacking before.

Iris, for a few moments, enters Sidney's fantasy.

> **IRIS:** You'll catch cold, Sidney. It's too early for games. Come to bed.
> **SIDNEY:** Look at the pines—look at the goddamn pines. You can taste and feel the scent of them. And if you look down, down through the mist, you will make out the thin line of dawn far distant. There's not another soul for miles, and you listen, really listen—you might almost hear yourself think.
> **IRIS** (surveying the realm, gently laughing): This is some mountain.

It's short-lived. Soon they need to move the car for street cleaning. But I'm willing to believe Sidney and Iris have got a chance. Politics will always fail us. But other people? Isn't this what happens sometimes? Someone else, if only for a while, joins our delusions?

» 59 «

NAOMI'S UNCLES, THEIR ENORMOUS HANDS SWOLLEN from work. They lived up the road from her grandfather's farm, in separate identical houses. This was outside Modesto. Together, along with running the farm now that the old man had retired, the two brothers operated a pesticide business. Uncle Jordan drove the spray truck; Uncle Lucas flew the crop duster. The duster looked to me like a First World War biplane. A landing strip, like a driveway to nowhere, reached out into the tomato fields.

In the early '90s a developer, wanting to build another housing development off I-5, offered Naomi's grandfather $9 million for the farm. The old man, like in some Clint Eastwood movie, gave the guy forty seconds to get off his property.

What was the point of being rich without land?

In the mornings, when it was cooler, we'd sit with the old man on the porch, the fat German shepherd asleep at his feet.

Naomi and I would eat tomatoes like apples, juice sweating down our faces.

The fact that we still weren't married wasn't merely an offense against the honor of the family, it mocked God's infinite mercy in broad daylight. Naomi's grandmother was named Cleopatra—and that's all anybody ever called her.

"It's on the calendar, Cleopatra, you know it's on the calendar."

Cleopatra sighed. Her sighs were monumental, slow avalanches of breath. Boris Pasternak has a line: "The Russian revolution broke out like a sigh held back too long."

Cleopatra's sighs were a counterrevolution.

"Whose calendar?"

They called me the fiancé.

I remember the mounds of dirt covered with tarp and tamped down by worn-out tires. I always meant to ask what this was for.

The orchards stretched in every direction, except west, which was I-5.

I don't think I'll ever see any of them again. At the time they tolerated me. They didn't have much choice. Naomi was the favorite granddaughter, the only daughter's only daughter. That she was a hippie who voted for Al Gore, an abortionist, could, in time, be forgiven, possibly. Everything, in time, could be forgiven, possibly, so long as Cleopatra retained the right to bestow it. Naomi slept in her mother's old room. I slept on a bunk in the storage closet. It wasn't a storage closet, it was a fairly large room just off the kitchen that they used for storage, but everybody called it the storage closet. Put the fiancé in the storage closet.

Cleopatra cleaned deep into the night. Dirt, like family, had to be kept in line. It wasn't until after two in the morning that I'd steal down the hall and lie beside Naomi in her mother's old bed, and even then we hardly moved.

"She knows," I said.

"Of course she knows."

"She'll murder us."

"She'll murder you. I've been baptized."

"What about after?"

"After what?"
"The consecration."
"Oh, that."

In the later afternoons, the sun drooping below the rows of trees in the orchards, Naomi's grandfather would go out on patrol. He volunteered with the Stanislaus County Sheriff's Office. He'd drive for hours, up and down his quadrant. Naomi made a short film of him rattling around in his pickup, bare elbow out the window, hat brim low just over his eyes. He never found any illegals. He could have rounded some up on his own farm since Jordan and Lucas hired them, as he had, too, in his day. That would have been cheating. Naomi shot the film in grainy black and white and the old man looked beautifully serene as he scanned the fields that bordered the highway.

We lasted two and a half years after a wedding in an apple orchard in Nicasio. Those ancient, craggled trees. We hired a harpist. My friend Lou, an Episcopal priest, officiated, which irked the Catholics as much as the Jews. (When I asked Lou to leave out Jesus, he said, "It won't bother Him.") I remember my father, in a white three-piece suit, stood up and gave a toast, his hair wisping in the wind.

And in the early mornings, having snuck from Naomi's bed back to the storage room just in time, I'd listen to those big uncles clump into Cleopatra's kitchen at 5 a.m. She made them coffee and buttered toast. The uncles never said much. Plans for the day, repairing some irrigation pipe, a trip to the True Value.

Cleopatra asking Uncle Lucas if it was all right to fly in this rain.

Uncle Lucas: "Ma, the prop flies under the weather. If you can drive in it, I can fly in it."

» 60 «

A GARY LUTZ STORY. IT DOESN'T TAKE UP A WHOLE PAGE. Like a tiny fortress. I've read it eleven times this morning. A dead sister's phone number. Her brother keeps calling it, again and again. This was back when we punched in phone numbers, each and every time, punched in the numbers. Lutz compares the muscle memory of that repetition to haiku. What's irrecoverable made tangible by the movement of fingers alone.

> I mean there was something physical about the
> way I kept ringing her up—

I've got my own numbers that my fingers still—
432-5181. 432-4474. 432-8719.

» 61 «

HER HUSBAND GREETED ALL OF US ONE BY ONE BY ONE. He thanked us for coming. "Thank you," he kept saying. "Thank you. Thank you." Some of us brought food, which was good because at least he wouldn't have to feed anybody. She was a colleague, a poet, erudite, tough. She wrote in English and French. She wore the French gently, never lorded it. And she was funny. She'd just turned fifty.

At the door he was thin, almost gaunt. As if she'd taken part of his flesh with her. All those months it took for her to die, so much work, for both of them. He was—is—a poet, too, and like her, a good one.

She'd been one of us. And what were we? We were all professors at San Francisco State. *Professors* always struck us as comic. Us?

We ate a lot, stuffed ourselves. It gave us something to do. We talked about the antics of the dean, gossiped, laughed. Like Ivan Illich's friends, we talked about work. Then: held our hands to our mouths, horrified.

The only saving grace of our presence, for him, may have been that at least our talk filled the house for a couple of hours. Among other things, she was a glorious talker. She was the rare person who, when she spoke up in a faculty meeting, you didn't dread it. The early 2000s. We'd meet up on the fifth floor, in the Poetry Center. A new building, allegedly built to withstand earthquakes of a certain magnitude. One day we were sitting around the conference table and the whole building started to sway and Stacy said:

"Anybody care to dance? Anybody?"

Stacy Doris. Her name was Stacy Doris. Quoting disembodied lines from "Knot iii.VII" do the poem no justice, but it might demonstrate the force with which she wrote:

> If people could feed on themselves which they
>   can
>
> Perhaps in this way all living's starvation
>
> Nobody needs to be alive to go on.

I keep Doris's work close, especially *Conference*, among the strangest, most provocative, and most unclassifiable books I know. A chorus of confounding voices that may or may not be birds. I'm not saying that I'll ever understand it, only that the book gives me a certain unnerving sense of comfort.

> The fate of those who aren't destroyed is to go
> home, over and over again . . .

I'm only someone who worked with her and liked her. We once served on a subcommittee together. Together we stood strong—very strong!—against restrictive circular requirements, whatever they were exactly.

And now I think of him, her husband, standing in the door of their house in the Outer Sunset, out on the Avenues, thanking us for coming and, then, later, after we were finally gone, having to face that night without her.

3 P.M.

Shadows lengthened across the garden, creeping up on glowing patches of colour still in sunlight.

—Eva Figes, *Light*

» 62 «

I'm at Verizon. "Dust in the Wind" is playing from speakers placed all over the store.

. . . all your money won't another minute buy

What happened to Kansas? Those dudes were poets.

All we are is dust in the

Is it me, or do some people actually like going to Verizon and talking into the maw of eternity about their fucking phones?

Now the Freedom Select Plus Plan comes with unlimited texts but not unlimited data.

But will 10 gig be enough?

That all depends on your usage, but with the Freedom Plus Your Ass Plan, you get—

At the same time, I'm waiting on questions about my own phone. How much to fix this cracked screen? Am I going to have to buy a whole new— And as I wait, I'm reading an essay by Mario Vargas Llosa. All I have to do is read a book at Verizon and in my own inglorious mind I'm the last Luddite intellectual on earth.

What about 20 gig?

That really depends on how much media you download.

. . . in the, everything is dust in the

Verizon is running a promotion on accessories. If you pay for six months of insurance on your phone, you get a hundred bucks' worth of shit you don't need. In order to take advantage of this limited offer you're required to sign up online for direct deposit. The Vargas Llosa essay has to do with the history of the novel in South America. He writes, "As you probably know, the novel was forbidden in the Spanish Colonies by the Inquisition."

I hadn't known that, actually. So interesting, Mr. Vargas Llosa. Why?

Samsung makes a comparable phone, which includes an X-87 FTQ camera for four hundred dollars less than Apple—

Don't Samsungs catch fire?

Oh, no. That was years ago. The children who make them have been retrained. Kidding!

The reason Vargas Llosa says that the Inquisition banned the novel was because the priests realized early on that fiction could be subversive. As a result, the very first copies of *Don Quixote* arrived hidden in an empty wine barrel. Those reading this forbidden book for the first time knew they could be jailed, tortured. Readers risked reading it anyway. The inquisitors, Vargas Llosa says, failed because they simply couldn't imagine how strong was the human appetite for escaping objective reality through illusions.

Kansas has given way to the Sheryl Crow song about the car wash.

Why does the light in here make me feel murderous and lethargic?

And something out of this fluorescent muddle takes shape: a memory of a moment, deep in *Don Quixote*, where the Don talks to Sancho about teeth. Don Quixote says there's nothing more valuable on the face of the earth than a molar. A tooth, Don Quixote says, is a sublime physical manifestation of the glory of God on earth. And I remember thinking of this scene as my father lay dying. At one point, his dentures popped out of his mouth and rolled down his chest.

My father who'd taken such good care of his teeth. He carried dental floss in his pocket. What happened to my father's teeth?

How strong the human appetite for escaping objective reality through illusions.

I was unmoved when my father died three weeks later, but when Don Quixote died, I wept.

In the last chapter of Book II, the Don disavows the stories, turns his back on illusions. His friends, the barber, the bachelor, the curate—after thinking Quixote was nuts for nine hundred pages now can't imagine a world where he isn't nuts. They all try to talk him out of sanity, beg him to reembrace his fantasies. You can't stop believing now! But Quixote's through with it. His return to his senses is final. He says his name is Alonso Quijano. He calls for a priest. He sends for the notary to make out his will. He forgives Sancho all outstanding debts and leaves him what's left in their jointly held account for traveling expenses. Sancho's response is: *Don't die, Master. It's lazy to die without somebody killing you.*

» 63 «

MY FATHER'S DELIGHT IN TAKING SPLINTERS OUT OF MY foot. Delight's mild. The man was ecstatic. He's lighting the match to sterilize the needle and getting ready to go to town. I've since learned that splinters do not lead to infection and certain death. That the little sprink of wood lodged in my foot would have wormed out eventually. Since learning this I've subsequently learned that this isn't necessarily always the case and that in some instances a splinter can actually— oh Christ, let the thing fucking kill me. With a match my father blacks the end of the sewing needle he carries in his shirt pocket. Lovingly he brandishes the infinitesimal sword. I scooch backward on my ass. Again, I can't sleep. And the tick of the clock in this otherwise empty room is my dead father coming toward me in flip-flops.

» 64 «

AFTER TWO IN THE MORNING. HOSPITAL BASEMENT. Gleaming just-mopped floors. The cafeteria closed. The vending machines behind a padlocked gate. I found a small chapel, empty, but the lights were on. I could have used some Cheetos but, I guess, if I've got no choice, I figure I'll take spiritual sustenance. I sat down on one of the folding chairs like the first guest at a funeral. There was once a cross in the center of the far wall. I could tell because of where the drill holes were. Nobody had spackled them over. It had once been a Catholic hospital. I took a book out of my bag to distract myself from hunger. Earlier that day a specialist had sauntered into my father's room and asked my father his name. My father couldn't talk, only whimper.

"His name is Ronald," I said.

"Ronny!" the specialist cheered, giving one of my father's bony knees a pat. "We'll have you dancing again in no time."

My father who never danced. Who has always been a Ronald. My father whose skin was hanging off his body like off a clothes hanger, who'd just shat the bed again.

In the chapel, I read the introduction to a book by an Argentine poet, Héctor Viel Temperley. After working for years in an ad agency in Buenos Aires, Temperley gave it all up, the job, the car, the apartment, the family. He declared himself a mystic. It was as if, he wrote, he'd been assaulted by a god, "a handsome god who looked like a Jewish sailor with a strong jab of jaw."

My father used to keep a sailboat moored at Wilmette Harbor. He never sailed anywhere. What he did on that boat was clean it. When he was through cleaning, he used to say, We'll set sail for Holland, Michigan, where all the chicks still wear wooden shoes. I was fifteen and full of rage. Even girls in wooden shoes held no interest. The state of Illinois, via a family court judge, had mandated that I spend every other Saturday with my father.

Wilmette Harbor is small and quaint. My father waited nearly two decades for the slip. He loved the place. He'd hail the harbormaster and discuss the barometric pressure, the heights of the waves. He'd tip the dinghy boys who motored us out to his 27-foot Cape Dory, handmade in Taunton, Massachusetts. I didn't give a shit. My father cleaned. He was never done cleaning. I'd lie on the bow slicked in Coppertone and try to get high off the fumes he was using to polish the brass and count the hours I had left.

I took the elevator back up to the fifth floor. I watched my father sleep with his eyes open, as if he were too exhausted to shut them. His breathing like a clotted drain. His new teeth had fallen out again and were resting on his chest. A show called *Primate Party* was on the television. I couldn't figure out a way to turn it off. I sat there in the pale light and listened to the baboons grunt. It isn't true we never sailed. We did go out on the lake a few times, and once got caught in a freak storm off the coast of Waukegan. In a matter of seconds, the wind shifted, the sky went from pale to soot, and the boat seemed to come to a wobbly stop, the sails flailing in every direction.

"Reef the jib!" my father shouted.

"What's a jib?"

"Lower the mainsail!"

"How?"

My experience with bad weather on a boat was not having finished *Moby-Dick* in Winnie Engerman's class. This book is a not a metaphor, she'd say. The white whale is not a metaphor, Ahab's stump is not a metaphor, and so on, and I sure as hell believed her now.

"Take the helm!"

"Me?"

I'd just gotten my driver's permit. But whatever I did, spun left, spun right, nothing seemed to have any effect, because we were rocking all over the place. My father scrambled to and fro across the boat, his hair wild in the gust, pulling, hauling, groaning, having a grand old time. A Jewish sailor!

Héctor Viel Temperley's *Hospital Británico* is about the time the poet was recovering from brain surgery while, in another hospital, twenty blocks away, his mother lay dying. He's in one bed. She's in another.

> Here she kisses my peace, sees her son changed,
> prepares herself—in Your crying to start all
> over again.

My peace? Never had much of it when it came to my father. But here's something. Weren't we once in irons off the coast of Waukegan? I believe I have the nautical terminology correct. We lacked all forward motion. My father and I were headed directly into the wind and the boat remained suspended, in irons, even as the sails and rigging whipped around like crazy. If it wasn't peace, at least, for a few moments, time itself was checked. After we survived, my father complimented me on my composure. I'd had no composure, I was just confused. I remain confused. What happened to my father's teeth?

» 65 «

WHAT DRAWS ME BACK TO THE STORY HAS NOTHING TO do with what happens. I know what happens. Outside, it's raining again, a silver March rain, the bare trees, a patch of old snow sits out in the grass like an island. It's early on a Sunday morning. Everybody's still asleep. I'm on the couch with the dog, reading Bernard Malamud's "Idiots First."

Mendel's got only a few hours left. He lives with his thirty-nine-year-old son, Isaac. We have different terminology now. Back then Isaac was a pure idiot.

Death also has a name. He goes by Ginzburg. And last night, deep in the night, Ginzburg visited Mendel to let him know his time was just about up. Mendel wakes in the cold dawn, having wasted precious hours sleeping. Isaac's awake. He's at the kitchen table playing with some peanuts.

As so begins a mad scramble as Mendel, with Isaac in tow, careens across Manhattan in an attempt to scrounge up the thirty-five dollars he needs to put Isaac on the train to an uncle in California. First, he hits a pawnbroker, who's in no rush. You know those people with all the time in the world while yours, your world, is collapsing?

> . . . a red-bearded man with black horn-rimmed glasses, was eating a whitefish at the rear of the store. He craned his head, saw them, and settled

back to sip his tea. In five minutes he came forward, patting his shapeless lips with a large white handkerchief.

Those shapeless lips. I can see them droop. I've never paused to notice his lips before. And something else this morning. I think of my first job. I was fourteen and worked at the Highland Park Sports Shop. Paul, the owner, had a little office at the back. He ate all day long. It was why I'd been hired. So Paul could eat in peace while I waited on customers. Eventually he'd come out, wiping his mouth with a paper towel, and finish a sale I'd already greased. These peripheral ghosts that lurk in other people's paragraphs. Paul? Paul what? I forget his last name if I ever even knew it. When he spoke directly to me, which was rarely, his mouth was full of kielbasa.

In Malamud's hammed-up Yiddish English, Mendel tells the pawnbroker:

> "Isaac must go to my uncle that he lives in California."
>
> "It's a free country," said the pawnbroker.

It's not a free country. The pawnbroker gives Mendel eight dollars for a sixty-dollar watch. What choice does Mendel have but to take it? He flees the shop, pulling Isaac, who's still playing with his peanuts, along with him.

Ginzburg, who's been following them, skulks in the shadows.

Next stop is Fishbein's mansion on the Upper West Side. Fishbein's servant opens the door and tells Mendel that Mr. Fishbein is dining at present. Mendel starts a fuss, refuses to be sent away. Fishbein appears, in a tuxedo, and tells Mendel he doesn't give to unorganized charities. It's not relevant here to mention that a guy named Fishbein stole my girlfriend in high school. Sweet-talked Emma right out of my skinny arms. Now he's a real estate developer. Maybe I take this story too personally.

> "Who's your uncle? How old a man?"
> "Eighty-one years, a long life to him."
> Fishbein burst out in laughter. "Eighty-one years old and you are sending him this halfwit."

Fishbein doesn't give Mendel a dime and the two are soon back on the street again. The wind blows mournfully. Ginzburg stalks.

Mendel digs a scrap of paper out of his pocket with another address but it's in Queens. Too far and there's so little time left. Instead, he drags Isaac to a nearby synagogue. He raps on the door of the rabbi's house next door. The wife answers. In stories like these the rabbi's wife always answers the door. She immediately tries to send Mendel packing but the rabbi himself peeps out from behind her, as gaunt as she is stout. All I need is thirty-five dollars, Mendel says. He may as well ask for thirty-five thousand. Still, the rabbi, from behind his wife, shoves Mendel a new fur-lined coat.

> "I've got an old one. Who needs two coats for one body?'
> "Yascha, I am screaming."

Like a screwdriver in the eye, the rabbi's wife's dialogue here. Yes, it's hammed-up Jewish vernacular but I used to have relatives, every Jew in America used to have relatives, who talked this way, as if contractions weren't invented. Yascha, I am screaming. But beyond this, isn't this the way you, too, have shouted in an extreme moment? A time when you've spelled out exactly what you were doing as if the person you were shouting at couldn't see you? *I am standing here and I am telling you that I love you. Can you not hear me? I am saying it and you will not hear—*

Mendel takes off with the rabbi's coat. With what it's worth, he's able to buy a ticket to California. Malamud skips this part. He cuts right to the train station platform. Mendel and Isaac arrive just in time, but, wait, the ticket collector refuses to let them pass.

> "But I see standing there still the train," Mendel
> said, hopping in his grief.

Hopping in his grief? An astonishing action. As if Mendel's body has become a separate character. Mendel can see the train right there in front of him. What else to do but hop since he can't move forward? I'm telling this as if Malamud hasn't already told it. But isn't this the way some stories are passed on, even when we we're only talking to ourselves? We tell even when the retelling has nothing on the original. I'm nearly out of breath. It's morning, early morning, and nobody in this house is awake.

Ginzburg and Mendel have, at this point, what I can only describe as a conversation about the inexorable law of death. Ginzburg tells Mendel that the grim reaper himself doesn't have the power to contradict the precise time of a single man's demise. Deal with it, he basically says. It's over. Curtains. Mendel goes for his jugular and, call it nonsense, but it's then (I buy it every time, and every time I'm shocked) that Ginzburg sees death itself reflected back at him in Mendel's raging eyeballs, and it's enough to freak the hell out of even him.

Wait, that's what I look like?

He backs off and lets Mendel put Isaac on the train.

And finally, there's this, a sentence that tolls with savage honesty.

> Isaac sat at the edge of his seat, his face strained
> in the direction of his journey.

Isn't this what we do? Don't we, always, leave our dead behind as we look toward Californias we can't even see?

» 66 «

BOOK OF MUTTER BY KATE ZAMBRENO. MUTTER. A good, humble word. We mutter the words we don't mean for anyone else to quite hear:

> I tried to nurse my mother. If I had known then what I know now—that she would die in mere months—I would have nursed her more. I would have abandoned myself to her. I would have given up my life, thrown myself on top of her, tried to crawl inside of her.

Zambreno's mother used to get up at 5 a.m. to start the housework. There's something about straightening and dusting and gathering up the clothes to be washed before the sun comes up, the silent optimism of it, as if you could set the world right before everybody wakes up and starts to unravel everything again.

After her mother's death, Zambreno searches the house, collecting traces.

> My mother's closet upstairs, the door on rollers, that familiar rattle and boom, the bedroom door was always closed. We were never allowed in there. An archive still carefully preserved, the

faintest of scents still clinging, a mixture of detergent, hand lotion, cigarettes . . .

She quotes Peter Handke's brief, infinite book about his
mother's suicide, *A Sorrow Beyond Dreams.* Handke is at
such a loss toward the end, he almost gives up. Paragraphs
give way to single sentences and even these become shorter
and shorter. Like Handke, Zambreno knows there are things
we have no business trying to say. Trying to explain one's
grief is to translate it, and translation, for all its necessity, all
its merits, can never be the thing itself. One imperfect solu-
tion: condense, distill, leave out.

On her deathbed my mother crying: Why
wouldn't the little girls play with Katie? Why
didn't anyone want to play with Katie?

The pain of being the kid nobody wants to play with. Of
ten I was this kid. Bad enough, but what about the mother
of a kid nobody wants to play with? So many ways to han-
dle it and all of them wrong. The wrenching thing here is
that decades later Zambreno's mother still isn't over it. Long
after Zambreno's forgotten about it (who the hell wanted to
play with those kids anyway?), her mother is still worrying.
I've got a daughter of my own and I stew, constantly and ir-
rationally, over whether she has other kids to play with at
school. The other day she mentioned she wasn't invited to
some Jessica and Amanda's birthday party (they're twins),
and for days I've been aching over it. Will my last words be
Why weren't you invited to Jessica and Amanda's party? Will
my daughter say: *What's he talking about? Who's Jessica?
Who's Amanda?*

Even memory is no match for the simple truth of one mother's, any mother's, biological breakdown. Zambreno:

> I try and make her comfortable. I give her little things to eat. Her body is so strange now. Curiously heavy.

Because even bodies ravaged by cancer can't help but be weight. Absence, too, of course is weight. The ultimate weight. Maybe this is why we always return to the things, even the smallest things, that outlast our people. In the hospital, Zambreno goes through her mother's purse and takes another inventory: A used tissue. Hand lotion. A lipstick never used. A wallet without money. Crumbling brown tobacco lining the bottom.

HERB? MY FATHER'S ELECTRICIAN?

A goliath of a man, a colossus. Not only an electrician, but also a plumber and carpenter. A handyman's handyman. Not a talker. My father came up to Herb's belly. He'd shout orders up at Herb like a person lost on a mountain, shouting without hope to the tops of the trees, and Herb would squint up as if tracking a mosquito he'd crush with a meaty finger. *Did somebody say something? Methinks I hear a wee voice.* It was a game they played. Who's in charge here? The big guy or the guy paying the big guy? Herb would come out to the house on Saturdays and do whatever needed to be done. In October, he installed the storm windows. In May, he took them down. He built the dog run, repaired fences, rewired the garage, paved the driveway. When my father changed his mind about the paving, it was Herb who brought a dump truck full of orange pebbles and slowly raked them out across the asphalt.

We hadn't seen him in upward of three decades when he showed up at my father's funeral. How he'd heard about it, who knows. We hadn't put it in the paper, the sad truth being there were so few people who might have been interested in showing up. There were three times more chairs than people. But Herb was present. Herb in the little chapel on the grounds of the cemetery squeezed atop a small plush chair.

It should have given me a little jolt of hope on behalf of humankind. This hulk in a dark blue suit. He wasn't sobbing; it
wasn't showy. Herb wept quietly. My father already burned
to ashes. On a table in front of the rabbi, in an urn, my father.
We stared at the urn. And after, after we took turns with the
shovel and dribbled some gravel into the small hole, Herb
hugged us, gathered us up, the few who of us were there. The
man could take two or three mourners at a time.

» 68 «

JUAN RULFO HAS A LINE MIDWAY THROUGH *PEDRO Páramo* when the dead narrator, Juan Preciado, says: "The murmuring killed me."

As she lay dying, his mother had told him to go to Comala and find his father, Pedro Páramo. Make that man pay, she said, for all the years he put us out of his mind. And Juan obeys, he goes to Comala to look for his father, but once he's there he becomes bogged down almost immediately by voices.

Voices of the dead? Voices of the living?

I'm inclined to believe they are the voices of the dead, as the dead speak more freely than the living. The living, if they are living, do more cowering in this book than talking. In any case, dead or alive, whoever they are, the voices kill off the narrator by page 61. Juan's mission is a flop. There's no dramatic face-to-face with the father. There's no catharsis. Sounds like actual life to me. Long-awaited confrontations—reckonings—usually take place only in our minds.

Juan Preciado may not make it out of Comala alive but his presence, the fact that he's there to hear the voices at all, is what cracks everything open. If not an effective avenger, Juan at least listens.

> "Oh, yes. I was nearly your mother. She never told you anything about it?"

"I wish I were a buzzard so I could fly to where my sister lives."

"It's only his horse coming and going."

"Then you don't want to see me tomorrow?"

"How cool the air is, Ana."

It makes me wonder if, at least in part, our survival depends on us *not* hearing the murmurs of the dead. Our own dead and everybody else's dead. The dead who once slept in the room we now sleep in. The dead who once walked the streets we now walk. And not only the murmurs of the dead, we can't afford to listen too closely to the murmurs of all the living. Because if we did it would kill us, too. If we were all as porous and open-eared as Juan Preciado we wouldn't make it past page 61, either.

For a while Juan Rulfo was a traveling tire salesman. He'd go around the country selling tires and pick up stories here and there. He also used to say he heard a lot of stories from his uncle. When asked once by an interviewer why he'd stopped writing, Rulfo said that when his uncle died, his stories dried up. Does it matter if this is true or not? I only know he must have been unusually attuned to the voices. Underground, aboveground. When he went silent, or tried to go silent, he may have thought he could finally be free of them.

» 69 «

IN CHAPTER 9 OF SHIRLEY HAZZARD'S *THE EVENING OF the Holiday*, Louisa, a graceful matriarch, an otherwise kind and generous person, has this thought about people in love:

> One would always think of oneself as being on the side of love, ready to recognize it and wish it well—but when confronted with it in others, one so often rejected it, questioned its true nature . . . was it merely jealousy, or a reluctance to admit so noble and enviable a sentiment in anyone but oneself?

Louisa is having lunch with Sophie, her niece, and Tancredi, an old friend. Sophie is visiting Italy from England. Tancredi is allegedly an architect though he never seems to need to work. These two have only recently fallen for each other. Louisa loves her niece, and Tancredi, well, he's practically part of the family, too. Of course, there are complications. Aren't there always? Tancredi's still married and there are two children. Or is it three? I forget. They're hardly mentioned. Anyway, why not be happy these two are happy? Why not simply wish them well? Look at them. Deep in that moony period when everything, including time itself, is weightless. Why not root for them? We know why. Because new love is always repulsive to the rest of us. Unless—need it be said?—we're one of the two. To be the third at a table with lovers in an early stage is a special hell, as intolerable as it is annoying. A third exists, if at all, only on the periphery. Louisa is sitting in her own house, at her own table, and she's nowhere. And the fact that Sophie and Tancredi are concentrating so intensely on her face only makes it worse. The sole respite is the storm that's begun to wail outside. It gives Louisa something else to think about. The garden, imagine all the destruction taking place in the garden.

Does Louisa take pleasure in the fact that she knows it won't last? She knows that soon enough Sophie and Tancredi will be knocked clean off their blissful perch, just as, outside in the garden, the urns are currently being blown off their pedestals. Do I take pleasure in it? Every patient sentence in this short burst of a novel brings us closer to the end of these two, of this time that isn't time. Maybe all readers are Louisa. All of us onlookers experiencing the passion at a remove. Resentful, and still we can't take our eyes off it.

» 70 «

KATIE HAD A DOG. AFTER I MOVED IN, THE DOG BECAME
my dog, too. Soon after that, we had a daughter. Fate spins
on less than a dime. Three years later the dog died. Another
three years passed and we had another kid, a son—he was a
bit of a shock. Eventually, we got another dog. But the new
dog will never be the old dog, and I remember sitting with
her—her name was Daisy but I called her Bud—in Precita
Park on one of her very last days, a cold one, San Francisco
polar June, and a guy came up to me and said, "Jesus, fuck!
Stevo!" I said, "Sorry, but I'm not Stevo." I reached down and
put my hand on the dog's head as if to say, If you'll excuse
me, I'm ministering. He said, "No, seriously, man. You look
identical to this dude I knew in college who came out west.
It's not even fair how much you look like Stevo." Then he
walked away and completely out of my consciousness until
this moment.

She'd been such a good dog. Her nose had started to crack
and bleed. Katie would rub moisturizer on it but it didn't
seem to help. She'd stopped eating. We had to force-feed her,
a process she didn't possess the strength to resist but the
look in her eyes told us both to drop dead. She was a big dog
and had always liked being outside so I'd hoist her up into a
wheelbarrow and roll her across the street to the park. I'd sit
with her on the grass while she tried to sniff the wind. Now I

think, what if I was Stevo, old college buddy who'd ventured out west? I was a Chicagoan living in California but I don't think it ever occurred to me that I'd come out west. Like I was some cowhand, a wrangler, and Daisy only recently retired from a long life of herding sheep. I'd sit there, those lost days, a parked wheelbarrow and a motionless dog. My hand on her head as she wheezed.

PABLO NERUDA:

> Do you remember when
> in winter
> we reached the island?

Again I can't sleep. Lying here on the couch, gnawing apples, the window open, this cold motionless air, I think of
places to remember. Do you remember when we? When we
reached—?

Bolinas? Purple Gate Road?

Like many of Neruda's poems, the one I'm thinking of
is rooted in the irretrievable. He tries, like us all, to conjure
what's gone with words, but this only reinforces just how far
away the island is now.

My old apartment on Twentieth and Dolores, after I'd packed
up all my stuff and you and I were standing in the middle of
that emptied room, all my stuff in boxes, the mattress against
the wall, and you said, Well, here's something. I'm pregnant.

What?

Let me put it another way. Pregnant I'm. Something
here's—

You don't look—

It takes a while. It's not like making a sandwich.

You say I stood up and circled the empty apartment. Then I opened all the windows and went to the one overlooking the park. Then I closed them, then opened them. And you say I went on doing that for a while, opening and closing every window, opening and closing.

Was it after that we put the mattress, which had been leaning against the wall, back on the floor? Because, without saying it out loud, we felt compulsed, and this is the word I mean,[4] to celebrate, to confirm, to assert, to proclamate . . .

It isn't as though at some point you start living your actual life. But there are times we might be forgiven for believing it.

It's February of a plague year. You're asleep. I'm crunching apples on the couch.

---

4   John McGhee is the best copy editor in America. All mistakes and weirdnesses my own.

» 72 «

Some nights I'd walk over to the farm and help
Abe out with the ducks. This was when Candace was in the
hospital and Abe was alone. They had something like forty
ducks and it was hell getting them inside their duck house
(formerly a dog house). You'd have to use a flashlight and
lead the ducks with it but first you had to figure out which
duck had designated herself the leader. I think it was always
a her. She'd have to track the light and follow it to the little
door, walk through it, be the first one inside. Ideally, then,
the others would follow. But given that the lead duck wasn't
very bright herself and the other ducks beyond stupid, the
whole process could take an hour or even two. Often the lead
duck wouldn't be able to track the light and so would wad-
dle right by the door, following the worn path that wound
around the duck house, all the other ducks stumbling close
behind. Three, four, five, six, seven times she'd miss the door
and the ducks would circle the house together, en masse.
They didn't squawk, they honked. Or the lead duck would
make it through the door but somewhere along the ragged
chain one duck would miss it and this new group would continue their way around again, this time without a leader. And
so—this mayhem went on until you were able to figure out
which one of the remaining ducks was capable of tracking
the light, and even then, after you got most of them inside,

there were always one or two stragglers who no matter what you did wouldn't go through the door and so became food for coyotes.

In the dark, Abe and I would talk about the ducks. Ducks, Abe said, have no muscle memory, or least mine don't anyway.

We lived on Purple Gate Road, across the road from Candace and Abe's. We'd left the city and found a place to be, to live, the three of us, Katie, the baby, me. It sounds like a joke but there was a gate and it was painted purple. One night a guy heading home from Smiley's missed the turn and plowed right through the gate. Head went clear through the windshield. So drunk he lived. When you're that loose, that floppy, you can survive anything.

If the wind was up you could smell the ocean from our yard. Also in our yard: groundhogs. They'd pull the grass down from below. I'd be looking out the window and suddenly a big hank of grass itself would, out of nowhere, shoot back into the earth. First time I saw it I thought I was eyewitness to a miracle.

Bolinas. We were never locals. Eventually, after three years, our landlord jacked up the rent by eight hundred dollars. Don't fall for a place you can't afford. An hour and fifteen minutes north of San Francisco, but you had to go over Mount Tamalpais. So it felt farther. The Miwok considered the place so sacred that they wouldn't live there. Anybody who tried was doomed. This has never stopped all the non-Miwok. First, the Italian fishermen who settled the place way back. Then, in the '70s, the poets from Haight-Ashbury who, the story goes, migrated north to clean up the coastline after an oil spill and never left. So antidevelopment, they used to call Bolinas the town that saved itself. Now the old poets ask: Saved itself for whom?

Realtors.

The November light. How in the afternoons the light in Bolinas would turn that thick yellow. I'd walk across the sewer ponds and want to die in that yellow light. Once, I even went over to the cemetery next to the Catholic church, thinking, If I can't live here any longer at least let me be dead here among these peeling eucalyptus trees. The fishermen and their wives in repose under crosses mingled with the newer, hippie graves, decorated with prayer flags and hubcaps. The eucalyptus: interlopers, too, natives of Australia. People say that when the town burns, it will be because of the eucalyptus trees, all those big fat matches waiting to be lit.

The chickens were easier. They bedded themselves down at night, and all that needed to be done was close and lock the hatches. Abe entrusted this job to me. The pigs needed nothing and didn't give a damn about anything and were ungrateful. But the ducks were a problem. I don't know why I think so often about the ducks. I don't need to describe them. They looked like ducks. But in the glare of the flashlight, I remember thinking they looked like fetuses. I enjoyed it, walking across the field to lend a helping hand to a neighbor with his recalcitrant waterfowl. Katie and Phoebe in the boxes of light behind me. Not that I did much. Sometimes I'd try to kick a duck back in line but mostly I just watched Abe wield the flashlight.

» 73 «

Chekhov at the Dunkin' Donuts in Grantham, New Hampshire. It's May 22, 2021, 7:15 a.m., and an employee in a surgical mask is walking among the parked cars distributing free samples of Dunkin's new breakfast sandwich. As far as I can tell, the new breakfast sandwich does not differ significantly from the old breakfast sandwich. The new one also consists of a sausage patty, cheese, and egg on a soggy, microwaved English muffin. Maybe it's a different kind of cheese? But we strangers, isolated, grateful, in our cars, grin and wave at one another as we chew our wedge of egg and sausage. There may be a pandemic. But there are free samples and there is Chekhov.

It's a radiant spring morning but Marya, the village schoolteacher, doesn't notice because she makes this journey to town once a season and hates every minute of it. And she knows that all the peasants, like Old Semyon, the carriage driver, gossip about her constantly. They think she gets paid too much, that she holds her head too high among them. *Twenty-five rubles? When everybody knows she could make do perfectly well on five?*

The road is muddy and rutted. Old Semyon talks, but only in random bursts. Some ruffian was arrested for the murder of Mayor Alekseyev.

"Who told you that?"

"People were reading about it in the newspaper at Ivan Ionov's inn."

They were silent again for a long time . . .

Marya and Semyon run into Khanov traveling in his carriage along the same road. A rich landowner in his forties, Khanov is a drinker with a haggard face and a sluggard look. But is he handsome? Absolutely, he's handsome. Khanov's carriage pulls up alongside Marya in her cart, and, after some chitchat, Khanov tells Marya that he's on his way to see a man named Bakvist. Then he says, "I've heard he isn't home!"

Not much else happens. At one point, the road is so rough that Khanov gets out and walks beside Marya. They talk some more. Eventually, Khanov gets back into his carriage and drives away to see Bakvist, who's probably not at home.

As they continue on, Marya and Old Semyon don't make any remarks. They don't, for instance, say, *Khanov is going to see Bakvist when he knows he's not home? That's strange!*

Hail Chekhov for letting the most minor of enigmas stand without comment.

And Marya? Well, her mind has already begun to wander back to the many ways she's insulted by the uncouth peasants she has lowered herself to live among. Then comes a paragraph where she can't help but fantasize about a different kind of life. Khanov? Him? *Be a wife?* She considers each day's dreary struggle. There's nobody to light the stove. The caretaker is never around. Her head always aches after classes. Exams, peasants, snowdrifts. She's become coarse and unattractive, awkward and clumsy, and lonely.

No one loved her, and her life was passing by mis-
erably, without affection, without the sympathy
of friends, and without any interesting acquain-
tances. What a terrible thing it would be if she fell
in love in her position!

Remarkable the distance, the abyss, between these two
sentences. It's also too funny to even laugh at it. Because he
knew. Most of us are miserable village schoolteachers. Given
the choice to escape, we'll remain. Imagine the calamities if
our stray daydreams came true.

» 74 «

ONCE, IN A HOSPITAL IN SAN RAFAEL, I LISTENED TO A heart monitor. Someone else's, not mine. I'd been admitted after eating three, it could have been four, pot cookies. Summer, Bolinas, 2013. Blade and Omar's place. A kid's birthday party. The kids were shrieking around like banshees. In the kitchen, on top of the refrigerator, were Omar's special "spicy" cookies for the mommies and the daddies. I wasn't eating the cookies for the dope. I was eating the cookies for the cookies. Give me a cookie, any cookie—

The hallucinations were mild at first. My mother kneeling to tie my shoe. And at first I was dimly aware of what was happening and understood I was seeing images, experiencing images would be a better way of putting it, but at a certain point I no longer knew that they were only images, or rather I knew and I didn't know and I knew. My mother was tying my shoes circa 1974 and at the same time I could see, clearly, my own currently bare feet rooted in the grass. The kids were zinging around me and at the same time there were still other parts of my what, consciousness?, multiple parts that were starting to fling all over in space and time. More faces, voices, visions. My ex-wife, my father, my third-grade teacher, Mrs. Gerschefski. My little dick is poking out of my purple corduroys. I went into the little outhouse Blade and Omar had built. A long story but they had no indoor plumbing. It was Bolinas. Blade and Omar lived in a tree-house. But the outhouse was outfitted comfortably and I stretched out on the tatami mat and tried to right my ship, but this was becoming impossible because I could feel my-self rotating like a rotisserie chicken and my ex-wife—why am I using this term? it sounds ridiculous, nobody's an ex-anything—Naomi, Naomi was screaming. No, I'm scream-ing. No, we're both screaming and it's like we're back on the tennis courts at Dolores Park in the middle of the night clawing at each other. No it wasn't like we were back at the tennis courts, we were at the tennis courts. And somewhere else, like in the next room of my brain, my father is lectur-ing me about keeping a car clean, how a clean car always runs better, and I start throwing food at him—I'm holding a bag of groceries—I throw some bananas, a can of creamed corn, and Naomi says, Because the membrane between the two rooms is so thin, even when you tell the truth it comes out a lie, and my father says, The floor mats, too, you have to vacuum the—and holy fuck, is that Mrs. Gerschefski na-ked? And somebody's pounding on the outhouse door and I shout, "One minute!" because I'm concurrently still aware that I'm a dad at a birthday party and that Katie's out there somewhere talking and laughing and so is our three-year-old, who's sprinting around—

I get up, fling myself out of the outhouse, and take off up the road toward our house. Because now I'm hyperventilat-ing and I've come to understand that what's really happening is that I'm having a heart attack. Die at home, I'm thinking. I spot someone's bike leaning against a toolshed. I take it and float, who needs pedaling?

—or if you don't have a vacuum, my father says, you can always take the floor mats out and beat them with a mallet . . .

A mallet? Where am I going to get a mallet?

Katie says that when she got home I'd turned on every faucet in the house and the bathtub was overflowing. I was on the kitchen floor moaning. I said I needed an ambulance. She told me I needed to chill, it's the cookies. I said I most definitely needed an ambulance pronto, and she finally said okay but I was going to be embarrassed tomorrow, and I said tomorrow I'm already dead, and this went on for a while because the ambulance had to come all the way out from San Rafael.

At one point I asked, "Where's the kid?"

"With Blade."

"Oh."

I went out in the yard and ran laps around the barn. Katie came out on the deck with a book and watched me for a while before she went back to reading. I tried to explain to her simultaneity, how I finally understood it now, how the past and the present, multiple pasts and maybe there's more than one present, too, and none of it linear, all of it played in a constant loop, everything that's ever happened, every day, every hour replayed, and if it wasn't for my heart imploding—

She looked up from her book. "You're very, very high," Katie said. "You don't have a single clue just how—"

"And Naomi and I are still on the tennis court, we haven't left, we're still—and my dad—"

"Good luck with your heart attack." She went inside, leaving her book on the chair.

Edibles, Katie told the paramedics, multiple. And they packaged me up and carried me away.

•

At the hospital, I needed no medical attention, though I think they may have given me an IV in order to be able to charge me for something. The ambulance ride alone turned out to be fifteen hundred bucks. A nurse with crescents under her eyes like little boats told me to take it easy, to try to stop talking, that she had patients to attend to, and then pulled that shower curtain around me, and I remember feeling cocooned in my bed, exhausted, not yet embarrassed, still amazed. The images, the voices, dissipating but still contemporaneous. That's when I began to listen to the intermittent beep . . . beep . . . beep of someone's heart monitor. Isn't a pulse a metaphor? A story we tell ourselves? If not the throb itself, the beep that speaks for it?

» 75 «

In December 1928, less than two years before his suicide in the Seine, Paul Celan wrote to his fourteen-year-old son, Eric:

> I am also happy for your reading. Gorky and Turgenev are naturally human, Gorky above all, the *tone* in which he narrates is richly authentic, the problems he goes at he truly lives them, everything starts from lived experience . . .

There's something almost unbearable about the delight Celan takes in his son's reading of a couple of old Russian graybeards. The poet's father died in a camp after being subjected to slave labor. His mother, because she was unable to work, was shot in the neck. Eventually Celan did succumb to despair. But maybe this is the point, that it wasn't that he cut his life short, it was that he hung on as long as he did.

Celan is sometimes described as a hermetic poet, and I take this to mean his work is so wrapped up in the cell of itself—cell as in prison, cell as unit of life—that it's inaccessible to readers, like me, who lack a secret key. Whether this is accurate or not, my own way of experiencing Celan has been to pull out a line or two and think about it rather than attempting some grasp of the poem as a whole.

There was earth inside them, and
they dug

I've read that Celan tried to distance himself from his
harrowing early poem "Death Fugue," and refused to allow it
to be anthologized any longer. He was infuriated that certain
German critics considered it a kind of fantasy when, for him,
"Death Fugue" was as close as he could get to facts. My understanding is that he came to believe that it even spoke *too*
directly, that it attempted to say out loud what he later came
to see as unsayable, or at least not sayable in such terms. Over
the years, my guess is, time itself fractured his memory, and
that fracture itself became truth. And he wasn't willing, anymore, to let stand the attempt to put it all together in a single
poem.

One late poem opens with these two stanzas:

that which was written grows hollow, that
which was spoken, sea-green,
burns in the coves,

in the
liquidized names,
the porpoises leap

I grope, pull on the strands a little. I read "that which was
written grows hollow" as a possible reference to his repudia-
tion of his earlier work. And "that / which was spoken" seems
to go in another direction: "sea-green, / burns in the coves."
The truth is I've no clue, but burning in the coves (speaking)
seems better than growing hollow (writing). Trying again,
I read the names as, possibly, those of his parents. So many

other liquidized names. But porpoises? What do porpoises have to do with anything?

I'm sitting on a picnic bench beside a little pond in New Hampshire. This is neither here nor there, but it's about a quarter mile from the birthplace of that singular American prophet, that seer of fantastically loony visions, Joseph Smith. It's late August and my two kids are swimming, yelling in the water, splashing. The kids, they dive and come up out of the water, their bare backs—like porpoises. I'm certain this isn't what Celan meant but it's how I'm hearing the line now. He was a father, too. *I'm also happy for your reading.* I watch my kids rise up out of the water. Out of the liquidized names. A new generation of children, carrying those very names, leaping. Am I anywhere close? Too optimistic?

THAT YEAR MY FATHER DROVE, IF I HAVE IT RIGHT, A Mercedes 280 Coupe. He worshipped that car. Took it to get washed every Saturday and supervised the washing. The guys at the car wash got a kick out of him because he'd take out his own chamois and join them in the buffing. Counterclockwise, he'd say, you rub a chamois counterclockwise. The guys didn't mind. It saved them a bit of work and he tipped decently. A silver two-door with red leather seats. The smell of that leather. Like the sweat of horses. Kennedy Expressway, just past Belmont Avenue. A siren. As if *siren* harked back to some old Greek meaning. To attract, to lure, to reel in, to hypnotize by exuding sexy charms. My father pulls off into the breakdown lane. Slow roll of blue and white light. How the light pierced the darkness, beckoning. He takes out his money clip and peels off a couple of bills. Hang tight, he says. Hang tight. Reaches into the backseat, grabs his furry hat, the one that made him look like a Cossack. Leaps out of the car and struts against traffic, fearless, toward the headlights. Nobody's going to shoot him. It's 1979. White guy in a three-piece suit, funny hat. Out the back window I watch. When my father reaches the squad car, he extends his hand. From the open window, another hand extends. The two hands shake. A few words exchanged, not many, and that's it. My father walks back and opens the door. He often talks about how well-made this car is, especially the doors. *You can tell by the way the latches sound when you open and close the door, that unequivocal force. The engineering, the Germanic attention to detail. It's in the doors. Germans are especially talented at doors.* Him grinning. *Follow me? Nobody's better at doors than the Germans. Now we buy up their cars.* He tosses his hat into the backseat. Cost me forty dollars, he says, used to be half that. The cop pulls out ahead of us without looking back. Not a bribe, my father says. Call it a professional courtesy. And we were flying along again from the Kennedy, merging with the Edens, as if hurled back into the night by a force beyond either of us, beyond engineering, and I felt, what—pride?

» 77 «

THIS OLD RAILROAD HOTEL IS NAMED AFTER CALVIN Coolidge's father. I'd always assumed the place was named in honor of the son until today when I read the plaque by the front door. Evidently, the father was an important Vermonter, too. Small population, everybody gets a plaque. Many passenger trains used to stop here in White River Junction. Now there's only freight, and once a day, running late, Amtrak. The other day Amtrak ran over a cow. Two weeks before that it was a car, and the driver fared as well as the cow. Neither lived.

These carpeted corridors are wide, built so that many people can walk up and down them. They are dimly lit and always empty. When I sit in this room with the door closed sometimes I hear muffled footsteps. I open the door and nobody's there. Only the motley line of plastic buckets and wastebaskets set out to catch drips from the ceiling. Blomp. Blomp. Across the hall is a masseuse. She seemed friendly when I ran into her, once, maybe a year ago, maybe longer. There's a whiteboard outside her office. This morning, at some point, because when I came in the board was empty, she wrote, *Be the energy you want to attract.* I've been sitting here for the past hour trying to imagine what it would be like to accomplish this. Out the window the sun lingers. Late

June, pandemic summer. The shadow created by the building across the alley is an oblong box. I've decided I will watch this box slowly shrink and disappear. Then, maybe, I'll go home.

At the hospital in Vienna where he was being treated for the galloping consumption that would kill him two and half months later, Kafka shared a room with a shoemaker named Josef Schrammel. In Reiner Stach's biography of Kafka, this shoemaker is described as a jolly man with a healthy appetite. The two patients quickly formed a bond. They must have, Kafka was only in that hospital for ten days. The shoemaker's family lived too far away to visit, and so it's safe to say that one of Josef Schrammel's last tethers to this life was a man named Franz, a skinny guy in the next bed. According to Stach, Kafka was rendered inconsolable by the death of the shoemaker, and, at some point, wrote this on a piece of paper:

> They killed the man beside me. They let him walk around with pneumonia and a 106 temperature. Wonderful the way the assistants were sound asleep in their beds and only the priest with his acolytes was there.

These three sentences are part of what have become known as "the conversation slips," brief lines that Kafka wrote during his last months because he could no longer speak. The pain in his throat was too excruciating. These slips of paper were collected and preserved by a friend of Kafka's, a Hungarian doctor named Robert Klomstock. Some examples:

Might I try a little ice cream today?

There was a bird in the room.

Please see that the peonies don't touch the bottom of the vase. That's why they have to be kept in bowls.

Every limb as tired as a person.

A day or two after the shoemaker's death, Kafka was moved out of the hospital in Vienna, a place he obviously hated, given the way his friend had been treated, and taken to a sanatorium outside the city. His last girlfriend, Dora Diamant, arranged the transfer. Most accounts I've read of Kafka's relationship with Dora suggest it was happy, in spite of his rapidly deteriorating condition. Sometimes she's referred to as his "child bride," but she was twenty-five and independent, having escaped her oppressive Orthodox parents. Stach writes that when the couple was driven to the sanatorium in an open car, Dora stood up the whole way to shield her lover from the rain.

In the sanatorium, Kafka's room had good light, a balcony, and a view of a brook and some woods. Dora was able to visit without restrictions. But word was getting out that his condition had taken a turn for the worse. Max Brod visited, as did Kafka's favorite sister, Ottla. Klomstock, Kafka's Hungarian doctor friend, arrived as well, to help Dora with the nursing.

To return to Josef Schrammel. If Stach's footnote, identifying the source of the note that describes the shoemaker's death as Klomstock—the collector of the "conversation slips"—is correct, then it stands to reason that Kafka wrote the note *after* the transfer from the Vienna hospital to the smaller sanatorium. Otherwise, why would Klomstock have had possession of it? (I'm in the weeds here, but we know that Klomstock, as I say, didn't come to see Kafka until *after* the move to the sanatorium.)

Why is any of this important? Why am I going on about this in the silence of this hotel as I wait for footsteps, shadows? Blomp. It is because, I announce to the mice who live in the air duct above my head, I've made a discovery. My mice are not scholars or even readers, though they do, from time to time, nibble on books and leave their tiny shits on my desk. Friends, Romans, Mouses, it's my contention, based on existing documentary evidence (due credit to Dr. Stach), that among the very last stories Franz Kafka wrote was one that consisted of three livid sentences. I say story because not only is the note about Schrammel vastly different in tone and content from the other conversation slips, it's about another person and what happened to that person. It's about a character and that character's fate. Are you with me?

> They killed the man beside me. They let him walk around with pneumonia and a 106 temperature. Wonderful the way the assistants were sound asleep in their beds . . .

Isn't it all there? The shoemaker quaking from fever. The indifferent snoring in their beds. A man's final breath. The priest and his minions in the dark. Last rites, the murmuring in Latin, as the shoemaker's friend looks on in sadness, terror, and increasing wrath.

Dusk

» 78 «

ELIZABETH TALLENT HAS A STORY CALLED "CIUDAD Juarez." In the opening scene, a couple in a car are on their way to Mexico. They haven't spoken to each other in five hours, not since Santa Fe. As they near the border, the wife reaches out, takes hold of her husband's wrist, and twists it toward her so she can check the time. The husband expects her to finally say something. At the very least some throw-away remark about how late it is. Anything. All that silence, how it's built up, enveloped these two in the car. Still, she doesn't speak, doesn't acknowledge his existence. Someone, without a word, seizing another's wrist to look at the time. A history of two lives in a gesture. Why mention it's late when they both know it's getting late? Isn't it always?

R<small>IGHTLY ACCUSED OF SOMETHING</small> I'<small>VE DONE</small>, I <small>RETREAT</small> with a single book. I haven't apologized. There will be no amends. And yet at the same time I'm making a vague, arguably disingenuous attempt to acknowledge, if only to myself, a particular crime among my many crimes. The felony of never knowing what I have. Bernadette Mayer's book-length poem in prose and verse, *Midwinter Day.* She wrote it, the whole book, on December 22, 1978. Before today I'd read only parts of it but this is a book to be swallowed whole, slowly, hour by hour, the way it was created. Therefore, my unpunishment has been to remain here in a chair in the public library in West Lebanon and read this day, this ordinary, sacred day, straight through (with a sandwich, cold coffee, and a Mars bar) in the distant hope that it might help me become a better person. I don't believe a book, any book, can do this but everything else I've tried has failed.

If there's one book that should be able to resist my inclination toward spastic hyperbole, it's *Midwinter Day.* And yet, here, now, to myself, in West Leb across from Advance Auto Parts, I'm going to proclaim, ordain, howl to the void, that this book constitutes the greatest celebration of family life ever written by an American.

Except, there's a pivotal caveat. Though Mayer's husband, Lewis, and their two young daughters, Marie and Sophia, are present on every page—there's breakfast, a trip to the library, lunch, dancing around the kitchen, making drawings, reading out loud, squeezed-in sex while the kids are at last asleep, toys on the floor, dreaming—this book, at its core, is a dense, 119-page record of Bernadette Mayer's fiercely *individual* consciousness across the seconds, minutes, hours of December 22, 1978. Thought after thought after thought, Mayer manages to remain as aloof from her family as she is at the center of it. An omniscient god who, even as she is busy offhandedly creating a multifaceted universe of the mind, also does the dishes and shops for beer and Pampers.

To quote *Midwinter Day* is like cutting out a vital organ. A kidney won't tell the story of a body or a soul. (A liver maybe.) And yet I've covered pages of this small black notebook with Mayer's lines. An hour ago I went to the bathroom. I took the book with me but forgot the notebook. It was naptime for Mayer's daughter, Marie. At the urinal, I scrawled on my arm:

Marie's asleep, the human race is saved . . .

Even worse is that any one of thousands of other lines of poetry and prose I could quote here run the risk of making Mayer sound merely quirky. But fuck it, this is what she sounds like:

We read Bready Bear. It's a story of a toy panda bear who decides he ought to live in a cave but he can't fall asleep there because it's cold and he's nervous and then he just falls down and can't move because he needs to be wound up again by the child to whom he belongs, a boy named

Thayer. I've had dreams that Rosemary becomes editor of the New York Times and has a son, that I am a marine and Bill Berkson is the head of my reserve unit, that Godard dies and comes back to life to make a movie, that Henry Miller shoots George Wallace, that Grace is in the Electoral College, that Picasso lives on Saturn, that Hawthorne turns into a white chicken . . .

That's only a taste of Mayer's crowded mind, and these batty shifts from Bready Bear to Rosemary (Mayer's sister) assuming the editorship of *The New York Times*, to Henry Miller assassinating George Wallace, to Grace (who's Grace?), to Picasso on Saturn, etc., etc., are examples of the sorts of leaps that characterize December 22.
Another:

We're only having spaghetti. Once on my mother's birthday which was April 4th, we went for a picnic to Clarence Fahnstock State Park and I refused to get out of the car.

Will Mayer give us an explanation of why she lurches from tonight's pasta to her mother's birthday picnic at Clarence Fahnstock State Park? Perhaps they had spaghetti on the picnic?
No, that's not why. They connect like they do in our actual brains. Meaning: they don't. Mayer knows what we all know, which is that often as not there isn't any rhyme or reason why one of our thoughts follows another.
A few minutes ago I had a vision of my grandfather's—Poppa's—bare feet. For a fat man, he had pretty small feet, or

so I thought as a kid. Nothing whatsoever about *Midwinter Day*, which I've been reading and thinking about for the past six hours, made me think of Poppa's feet, and his feet aren't related in any way to any of the above sentences. I simply saw them a few minutes ago. Feet I haven't seen in more than twenty years, suddenly, there they were.

I have no evidence to support this but I'd say Mayer wrote with one hand and held the kid's Bready Bear book in the other. That her notebook was open on the counter as she poured the spaghetti and the boiled water into the colander. That as she let the water drain into the sink, she wrote a line or two or three. Or while she was chopping vegetables. Or while enjoying that quick fucking while the kids were finally asleep. Hang on, Lew, I just thought of something.

Mayer states directly that she seeks to prove that a single day has everything in it. At the same time, she's not going to force anything particular upon it. The day will bring what the day will bring. By everything, I think she means possibility. Doesn't every given day, at least in theory, have that? Mayer also describes the book as an attempt to write an "introduction to love." That this December day, in spite of all its aggravating, time-sucking details, the meals, all the meals— multiply each by four—"divided into the light a length of a day is measured more in numberless meals"—is if not love itself, at least, yes, its introduction. Laundry, the water bill, the phone bill, the heating bill, more laundry. Unpaid bills and laundry, if you think they can be separated from love you don't live in the world.

And somewhere amid all this, Mayer writes (I can't find the page) that Tolstoy once leaped onto his father-in-law's shoulders in a moment of joy.

The woman in the next chair is snoring, peacefully, a

couple of plastic grocery bags at her feet. There's a guy pretending to read a magazine, and that's not water in his water
bottle. The hushed way people talk in the library, like it's a
morgue and all the books are dead people. Except the librar-
ians, who all shout like train conductors. You read somebody
for six straight hours, you start seeing through their eyes. I
love the hushed voices, this strange anachronistic reverence
for the books. Most people are here to use the public com-
puters. There's a sign-up sheet. Twenty minutes maximum
if someone is waiting. Please No Pornography. Twenty-five
cents per page for black-and-white prints. Seems high. The
sounds of chairs being pulled in and out, the clack of shoes
walking away. This library is chronically underfunded. There
have been two overdose deaths in the bathroom in the past
three months. I read that in the *Valley News*. Outside it might
still be raining. I haven't looked out the window in a long
time. Inside this book Mayer is still busy, the day being not
over.

> I was going to tell about garbage
> and how taking it to the yard . . .

I do wonder what Lewis, the husband, who's also a poet, is
doing all day. He must be writing poems. Something else occurs to me, and maybe this is obvious, but this book is not remembered. It's life in real time. This is not a memorialization
of family; it *is* family. Memory is only one aspect; the momentum comes from the present action, from the routine of
this particular day. It isn't December 21 or December 23. But
think about it: All this in a single day? I have this persistent
worry about what will happen when I run out of things to
remember. Will I have to live? I wish I were kidding. Mayer

is back from the 7-Eleven where she's gone out for the beer and diapers. Now she's sitting at her desk in a down jacket.

All the windows are frozen shut.

All the windows in Bernadette Mayer's house are frozen shut. I'm still sitting here in West Lebanon. My own family is at home across the Connecticut River and everything I've squandered encloses me like a fist.

» 80 «

ALWAYS THE YEARS UNFURL BACKWARD, BOLINAS 2012, the afternoon sun behind the clouds. The clumps of dry grass outside the window. It was late spring, wasn't it? Hard to define a Northern California spring. The wind lets up a little. I assume at a certain point flowers start to blossom. I can't pretend to know. Was it a Tuesday? Nothing special about the day. Why don't I remember more of them?

We were in the kitchen, the kid, finally, my god, at last, asleep, and I said, Do you want?

You shrugged. Sure, why not?

Upstairs you said I was dawdling. You said, Let's get the show on the road. Any second, she's going to wail—

I said, I'm luxuriating in the future before it's—

You said, Where's the dog?

Under the bed.

You leaned over and tried to coax her out. Come, Daisy, come, come. She won't. I'll get her a treat.

We're out of treats, I said.

I just bought some.

Phoebe gave her the entire box.

No wonder she's farting so much.

•

234

The spring light in Bolinas, a heavy greenish light. Walking the path through the sewer ponds, even the smell of an entire town's shit had a sweet green stench.

Come on, let's—
    You want to terrorize her?
    Who? The dog or the kid?
    The kid's asleep, the dog—
    She's fine, come on, let's get this show—you think the dog hasn't heard us?
    You don't want to talk?
    Okay, let's talk.
    You want to talk?
    You just said you wanted to talk.
    I knew a guy who ate pizza off his wife's chest.
    What?
    Actually, it wasn't him. It was his wife's chest but not him. She was having an affair and this guy was doing surveillance. He planted a camera in their bedroom and that's what he saw on the recording, the two of them having a pizza lunch—
    You want to do that, whatever it is you're talking about?
    No, I'm just—you know what the problem with sex is?
    Where do you want me to start?
    It makes us anonymous. We become like everybody else. There's only so many ways—
    Shit, the baby.

» 81 «

WHEN HE WAS GROWING UP, MARILYNNE ROBINSON's Jack Boughton used to sneak out of the house on Sunday mornings before church. He didn't want to be an embarrassment to his preacher father. It wasn't that he, self-acknowledged bad seed, wasn't wanted, in church or anywhere else. His father, along with everybody else in the family, was only trying, desperately, to find a way to love him that wouldn't induce him to run the other way.

No, it was because he could be so charming. It's this that repulsed him. He'd stand outside with his father, as the son of a reverend was expected to do, as were his brothers, Teddy and Luke, and shake hands with the parishioners. And Jack would smile a ridiculous hundred-watt smile. He couldn't help overdoing it, to make up for what he couldn't seem to feel. He came from a loving family, why couldn't he simply love them all back? And his father would become uneasy and wrap an arm around him so that Jack could feel the tremor of embarrassment in his father's muscles, and it was this, not his already well-known reputation as a truant, drinker, cavorter, petty thief, that made Jack skip church. He wanted to spare his father this after-church performance. All the things we do, have always done, in order to dodge an awkward confrontation with love.

» 82 «

THIS MORNING I WATCHED MY DAUGHTER—WE WERE late again—steel herself just before she opened the door to the school. I only saw her face in profile but I could tell there was something different about her expression, a pained look I didn't recognize.

I called out to her. I wanted to say, No big deal, so you're late. Who cares? Miss Pelly's cool.

She heard me, I know she heard me, because her face tightened even more. She pulled the door and went in. I watched the door float open for a moment before closing.

» 83 «

THE POET VIEVEE FRANCIS—WHO WORKS ABOVE ME, IN
the clock tower of this old hotel—told me this on the sidewalk today, in front of the post office. She said that the reason
the final lines of Robert Hayden's "Those Winter Sundays"
are so memorable, the reason they are so embedded in our
brains, in our hearts, has to do with Hayden's choice of em-
phasizing O sounds in *What did I know, what did I know / of
love's austere and lonely offices?* It's about the repetition of the
sounds, Vievee said. "By the end of the poem we are moaning and we don't even know it."

» 84 «

IN HIGH SCHOOL, I WAS A LIFEGUARD AT ROSEWOOD Beach. I'd sit up there in a tall chair, a chubby non-Adonis in my mother's mirrored sunglasses, and I was such a stupid doof that I'd watch the waves and wonder if anybody ever was going to start drowning.

» 85 «

LEONARD FOUND HER WALKING STICK BY THE SIDE OF
the river, but it wasn't until three weeks later that her body
surfaced. Some teenagers on bicycles found a corpse washed
up on the riverbank. That's when they discovered what was
in her pockets. I've always heard it was multiple stones. It
was only a single heavy stone. Such details shouldn't matter.
Multiple stones? One stone? Weight is weight. I'm doing what
countless others have done before me, picking over her body,
what was left of it. By March 1941 she'd mostly stopped eating.

I've been skipping ahead in biographies lately. It's less
morbid curiosity, though I'm guilty of this, too, than a fac-
ile theory that toward the death comes distillation. That as
a person deteriorates, physically or mentally, they (or their
biographers) are more likely to cut to the chase and tell me
what I need to know. Today is no different than any other
day lately. I'm still largely cut off from other people although
I don't mind very much. These hours I spend alone in this
old hotel are a strange gift. A couple of cooks, on break from
the restaurant, are down in the alley. I can't hear what they're
saying through their masks, only their laughter. Also, the
wind moans a little through the warp in the window frame.
The paper towel I stuffed in the gap isn't doing any good.

In the last chapter of her biography *Virginia Woolf,* Hermione Lee writes:

She could swim, but she allowed herself to be
drowned.

Lee didn't write this lightly. I imagine it rattled her,
even after all the years she spent digging into every angle of
Woolf's life, even when of course she knew it was coming.
She had to find a way to write it. The sentence above ends the
paragraph that details all that is known about Woolf's last
day, including the text of the letters she wrote to Leonard.
I appreciate how Lee just says it and leaves it be, allows a
reader free fall into the space break that follows. Yet there's
something about the use of the word *allowed* that suggests
passivity. Her bottomless and recurring despair wasn't a secret to anyone close to her, and this, too, has been picked
over by many biographers, including Lee. There were the in-
stitutionalizations and at least two previous suicide attempts.
Even so, *allowed* feels limp given the circumstances. On the
other hand, as I sit here staring at the sentence, the first part
of it—*She could swim.* This gets right at it. She could. She
could swim.

At some point in the weeks after, Leonard Woolf wrote on a
scrap of paper:

> I know that V. will not come across the garden
> from the lodge, and yet I look in that direction
> for her.

Down in the alley the cooks are still laughing.

» **86** «

CHICAGO, FEBRUARY. THE TALL CEMETERY TREES. PALL-bearers aren't called upon to do much lifting anymore. It must have to do with liability. Sue the mortuary over your hernia. The casket rode on a kind of gurney. We pushed it a bit, together across the frozen ground, and then the three gravediggers took over, yanking the gurney over the rougher spots—roots, stumps, other graves.

We gathered under the small yellow tent in the wind in lightly blowing snow. Aside from the plastic chairs there were two chairs covered over with plush velour, little thrones in the front row. Rosehill is massive, the largest cemetery in Chicago. It stretches west from Ravenswood to Western Avenue and north to south from Peterson all the way to a diagonal street called Bowmanville. Rosehill is not in a neighborhood, it *is* a neighborhood. Still, you could drive by the place for years and not notice it. Cemeteries are for everybody else.

I watched the three gravediggers. They stood, hatless, beside the casket, snow gradually whitening their hair, as they waited for the rabbi to finish. A boyish rabbi. I was disappointed that he wasn't more wizened.

Weep with him, ye who are distressed of heart.

Rosehill is nondenominational. The three gravediggers have probably heard every eulogy there is. They stood there, motionless, like brothers to the trees. My mother and my nine-year-old daughter were sitting in the plush chairs. My daughter reached for my mother's hand as my mother shook.

The grave workers lowered my stepfather with the help of a small portable crane. One of the men operated the crane while the other two guided the casket with gloved hands. The casket hovered and we all watched it, attached by a hook to a cable. There's no elegant way to do it. The noise of the crane was like a lawn mower. The men had to lean precariously over the grave in order to line up the casket with the rectangular hole without falling in themselves. I'm sure this has happened, that there are many stories.

They used to talk, my mother and Dan, deep into the night. I'd be trying to sleep in the guest room at the end of the hall and the two of them, at three, four in the morning, would be chattering like birds. Forty years of talk. We all fear the silence now. Dan was eleven years older and into his nineties. My brother and I had tried to not think about it. You can't pre-break your heart.

And then phone calls from the hospital, last-minute flights. The airlines have done away with bereavement discounts. They know we'll pay anything, put it on a credit card and worry about it later. Suddenly we all know what to do. We make more phone calls. We make arrangements.

My daughter knows to reach for my mother's hand.

I've had a few father figures, only one father, but also a stepfather who not only put up with me, he accepted me as his own, enfolded me into his life. I was welcome to the party. Grab a drink and join us . . .

They lowered Dan without incident. There was no audible thud. Inaudible, yes. And the men, the three men, backed away. They left the equipment and backed away into the trees.

IN THE "PHOSPHORUS" CHAPTER OF *THE PERIODIC TABLE*, Primo Levi recounts that, before he joined the partisans, he worked in a lab in Milan. It was there he fell in love with a fellow chemist named Giulia.

Giulia was funny, smart, straight-talking, irreverent, fearless, sexy—and taken.

> And what about me? No? No girls? That's bad.
> She would try and help me out there, forget about
> the racial laws, a lot of nonsense anyway, what
> importance could they have?

The two of them attend a matinee together. After the movie, Giulia asks him to take her home. Levi says he's sorry, he's got a dentist appointment. Another time Giulia orders him to ride her on his bike to her fiancé's parents' house— immediately. These parents have rejected her, forbidden the marriage, and Giulia wants to tell them off to their faces. Levi does as he's commanded. As he rides her on the cross-bar across Milan, Giulia tells him that her fiancé's parents think she's not pretty enough. Levi blurts: "What idiots! You look pretty enough to me." It isn't great but at least it's a start. Giulia's having none of it. She says:

"You're a fool. Go on, keep pedaling. It's already late."

Primo! Don't you see this is it? Here's your opening. Stop the bike! Tell her how you feel about her, just blurt it out. It need not be said. We fumble our biggest moments. Primo Levi, majestic chronicler of Auschwitz, is only a timid lover on a bicycle. It's so ordinary you want to fall to your knees.

Giulia does marry the fiancé. She leaves the lab. Within the year, Levi and a group of friends head up into the mountains to fight the Fascists. None of them were very gung-ho about it. Levi describes them as the most disarmed partisans in the Piedmont. They weren't guerrilla fighters; they were a band of want-to-be artists who wrote poems. (Well, most of them wrote poems. Levi says that Ettore, who was studying to be an engineer, considered poetry undignified.) The friends surrendered without firing a shot. They were all taken into custody. And since the Fascists, in cooperation with their German occupiers, had at that point begun deporting Italian Jews—the racial laws were now being enforced in earnest—soon enough, within a few months, by October 1944, Levi was in Poland and, along with an anonymous mass of others, filing past "the commission" that would, with one quick look, decide whether he lived.

And it was at that moment Levi had a titanic, if brief, battle with himself. He nearly prayed to God. In his final book, *The Drowned and the Saved*, he writes:

> For an instant I felt the need to ask for help and asylum.

He resisted. The moment passed. He did not waver for more than a second or two, before he committed himself to fate, without appeal to any higher power. You don't change the rules at the end of the match or when you're losing.

You don't?

I'm lying here on my back in the hotel, on the floor, in the half dark of an idealess afternoon. I'd have crumpled. It goes without saying. So many Jews like me, so many of them stronger than I'll ever be, crumpled. But before that, if I'd had a few seconds, I'd have begged God's last-second intercession. I'd sure as hell have begged the God I don't believe in. What would I have to lose?

Forgive this sacrilege. I can't help questioning whether Levi's anecdote doesn't fit too snugly into his argument. *Pray? Nope, not me. I was above it.* It makes Levi so un-Levi-like, the hero of his own story.

> A prayer under these conditions would have been not only absurd (what rights could I claim? and from whom?) but blasphemous, obscene, laden with the greatest impiety of which a non-believer is capable. I knew that otherwise, were I to survive, I would have to be ashamed of it.

Over and over, I read these lines. I ping-pong from questioning to accepting, accepting back to questioning. Levi goes on to say that he's not evoking any kind of superiority, that in his opinion, on the whole, believers fared better in the camps because their universe was more encompassing, that believers had, in effect, something to look forward to beyond what was happening to their bodies in the present moment. "Their hunger," Levi writes in a sentence that goes on for miles, "was different than ours."

A case for believing? Absolutely. But Levi had never been a believer and he wasn't going fake it. Not then. The crucial words above might well be *were I to survive*. I wonder if the refusal itself is what saved him that first time he was saved. That the strength of the refusal was visible on his face to "the commission." Or rather visible somehow in the way he held his body because of course they wouldn't have looked at his face and into his eyes. What use was a face? Maybe a single glance at his body, at the way he was holding his body, was enough for them, whoever they were, to catch an inkling of the force he'd just asserted. *Here's one with at least another day of work in him.*

» 88 «

YEARS LATER, AFTER AUSCHWITZ, AFTER THE WAR, LEVI would, once again, see Giulia.

> She has had many hardships and many children; we have remained friends, we see each other every so often on the street in Milan and talk about chemistry and other reasonable matters. We are not dissatisfied with our choices and with what life has given us, but when we meet we both have a curious and not unpleasant impression (which we have both described to each other several times) that a veil, a breath, a throw of the dice deflected us onto two divergent paths, which were not ours.

I linger over the phrase "chemistry and other reasonable matters." He seems to mean there was some invisible line separating the things they could talk about from the things they couldn't. Chemistry, work, children—those subjects were all right. I get it. You're Primo Levi and you see someone on the street, someone you once loved, where to even begin? *Well, after I was nabbed trying to fight the Blackshirts with a butter knife and some poems, I was deported to . . .*
The conversations the two were able to have, the ones he

alludes to in parentheses. The way these two talked with each other about fate and chance. A veil, a breath, a throw of the dice. And not only his hardships, but hers.

What must it have been like to look into Giulia's face and see that before-time?

» 89 «

ANDRE DUBUS HAS BEEN DEAD TWENTY-TWO YEARS.
This morning I read "Sunday Morning" from his final collection, *Dancing After Hours*. Something about reading the
sentences of someone you've loved. Every line is a message
from the grave.

> Her fear could not have been that sudden, but in
> memory it seemed so, as if she had waked to it
> one ordinary morning.

Tess has just spent the night with a man she's met at the
supermarket. It's Sunday morning, quiet, the window's open,
there's a breeze, and Tess and Andrew are in bed drinking
coffee. They talk about going to breakfast. Andrew wants to;
Tess is evasive. She's got something she needs to say. And
without preface or warming up to it, she tells Andrew, this
person she doesn't know, that a friend of hers was murdered
by her husband.

> "Jesus, in a fight?"
> "No. He never drank. You'd see them together,
> and you'd think, *That's how a couple should be.*
> He watched her when she talked. He actually lis-
> tened to her. No: he planned it."

The husband shot the friend in the face while she was three months pregnant. Maybe it's a thing you tell someone in order to watch how they hear it. Andrew asks if it was about another woman. Tess tells him no, that wasn't it, either. He wanted to open a nightclub. Andrew, hoping to change the subject, offers to run to the corner store for cigarettes. Tess doesn't want cigarettes. She doesn't want breakfast. She's not done talking. A couple of weeks before the murder, she says, she and her friend had lunch. The friend happened to mention, between sips of soup, that her husband had taken out more life insurance on her. She didn't know why.

> And she held the spoon there for a moment, look-
> ing at me. Then she waved her left hand past her
> eyes, just once, like she was fanning smoke away
> from them.

Is there anything we won't refuse to see if we don't want to see it?

So many things I never had the chance to ask him. After an accident—Dubus was run over on I-93 north of Boston and lost one leg and the use of the other—he couldn't write fiction. It took him years to find the silence again.

I think of his mornings, working at the small wooden desk in his bedroom. He writes by hand but mostly he doesn't write at all. He waits. He backs his wheelchair up a little and rubs his face because he sees it now. A hand, just once, waving away smoke that isn't there.

A DECADE AGO, IN FALL RIVER, MASSACHUSETTS, MY mother's hometown, the water in the Vietnam Veterans Memorial Pool was so murky that a woman drowned without anybody noticing. She'd gone down the water slide and hit her head. She sank and remained unseen until, two days later, her body rose to the surface. Some boys who'd climbed the fence to swim after hours, at night, discovered her floating.

I don't tell this to humiliate Fall River. Plenty of people have already done that. The story of the woman who drowned unobserved in a crowded public pool ricocheted in the media around the world—for a day.

My grandfather Fred loved Fall River so much he didn't tolerate anybody making fun of it. He collected books about King Philip's War, which was fought in and around what's now Fall River. After some pilgrims with firearms ambushed King Philip at his hiding place in Misery Swamp, they put his head on a spike and made a parade out of it. I read this in one of my grandfather's books when I was a kid. They did the same thing to King Philip's staunch ally, the chief of the Pocasetts, Queen Weetamoe. They chased her into the Taunton River. It's said that Weetamoe couldn't swim, but even if she could have, the currents in the Taunton would have been so strong she'd never have made it across. When they dredged her body up, they put her head on a spike, too.

Many things in Fall River are christened after these two. A mill, a cigar company, and a national bank, all were named for King Philip. Weetamoe got a street. My mother grew up on it. In this country, we murder; then we honor.

The drowning at a public pool in 2011 was the result of a grotesque confluence of facts. The lifeguards weren't well trained. The pool was perennially underfunded. That summer, the rec director made the decision to fill the pool without first cleaning out the dirt and dead leaves and debris that had accumulated during the off-season. He was under the gun to open.

Failure after failure. The dirt, the dead leaves. Open the pool on time. It was hot, so hot. Fall River is a cauldron in summer.

Marie Joseph. The woman's name was Marie Joseph. She was a mother of five and worked as a housekeeper.

In *As I Lay Dying,* Darl doesn't witness his mother's death. Pa has sent him and Jewel to town with a load of lumber. The load is worth three dollars. Three dollars is three dollars. And yet it's Darl who gives us the minute details of her last hours. Faulkner knew that you don't need to be present to see, that vision is as much about imagination as it is proximity. It's Darl, who's not there, who tells us that Addie Bundren watches out the window as Cash saws the planks for her coffin in the failing light.

> The sound of the saw is steady, competent, and
> unhurried, stirring the dying light so that at each

stroke her face seems to wake a little into an expression of listening and of waiting, as though
she were counting the strokes.

The boys climbed the fence and stripped off their shirts
and jeans. It must have been dark but the streetlights along
Eastern Avenue would likely have enabled them to see the
shape floating on the surface of the water. It wasn't a scene
out of a horror movie. It suddenly got very quiet. The boys
whispered to one another. They knew the woman bobbing in
the water was dead and that there was nothing they could do
for her, not in this life anyway. A few moments of stillness as
they stood there in their underwear at the edge of the pool.
Then they got dressed and climbed back over the fence and
called who needed to be called.

» 91 «

In "Blackbirding on the Hudson," Yusef Komunyakaa says he doesn't know birds, he knows New Jersey. How
blunt and elemental this is. In our bones we know what we
know. The poet is in Poland, but it's there, on a shelf, he
finds a book by Robert Lowell. One of Lowell's poems sends
him back to the Hudson River. One line and we're displaced
completely.

I think of Lake Michigan in all seasons but especially in
winter. This past February I walked with my grief-shocked
mother on the beach by the sewage plant. There was a tangle
of icy, stunted trees along the edge of the beach. They looked
as though they'd been blasted white by a high-powered paint
gun. They didn't look like trees, they looked like grotesque
sculptures of trees.

My mother groans silently into the wind.

"Look at the trees, Mom."

"I see them."

Komunyakaa writes:

I have also gone where love has taken me.

This may say all there is to say. We all go where love takes us, whether closer or farther. If the grief of a single loss in a single house on a single street in Highland Park, Illinois, is incalculable, then how is it possible to account for the losses on the rest of the street, the town, the county, the state . . .

Komunyakaa:

I still believe water is memory.

And in this poem, this devastating poem, Komunyakaa descends deep into the guts of loss and generations and generations of mourning, from the Middle Passage to yesterday and tomorrow, and the only way to respect it is to find it and read it. It's in *The Chameleon Couch.*

My mother is so small now. When we hug there's little of her to hold me up. We walk across the frozen sand. My Massachusetts-born mother has now lived within a mile of Lake Michigan for six decades. She leaves me and walks to the edge of the water. The waves shove up chunks of ice, each time reaching a little higher up the beach.

I've heard it said that lakes have no tides. I dispute this, oceanographers.

There are days I crave the lake, when I look east and there's nothing at all in that direction but trees and unfamiliar mountains. When I was small I'd go down to Millard's Beach and lie in the shallows and let the current wash over me, and I'd put my ear to the bottom and listen to the way the tiny pebbles seethed as they tumbled back and forth beneath the water. We walk the beach where love has taken us, my mother and me. February sun over Lake Michigan. There's no warmth in it. It's fake as varnish.

» 92 «

So many accounts of Chekhov's death, many of them exaggerated, some outright bogus. The only indisputable thing is him dead at forty-four. That's etched in stone in Moscow. I like to read them anyway. I'm not alone. Chekhov death fanatics abound. Is it some attempt at slowing it down, of trying to hold on to him a little longer?

His last sip of champagne. The whole thing about the popping of the cork, I forget what exactly. The enigmatic final words, *Has the sailor left?* Wouldn't it be wonderful if he had said them? What sailor? Where'd he go?

His wife, Olga Knipper, the actress, wrote that a huge black moth careened around the room, crashing into light bulbs as he took his final breaths. She, of course, was present in the room but I don't think Olga Knipper was above creating myths, either. They had so little time together, less than five years. Is there a greater myth creator than grief?

In 2018, a team of scientists examined the proteins in the bloodstains of the shirt Chekhov was wearing when he died, in an effort to determine the precise cause of his death. The shirt had been preserved as a holy relic and he'd coughed up so much blood.

This morning I've been wandering through Gustaw Herling's *The Journal Written at Night*, a book that took thirty years to finish and consists of essays and fragments that read like private messages. Herling, a member of the Polish resistance in the '40s, was sentenced, by the Soviets, to hard labor in a prison camp near the Arctic Ocean. But wait, weren't the Soviets and the Resistance on the same side against the Nazis? The bizarro reason: Herling, in Russian, sounded too much like Göring. After his release, Herling spent much of the rest of his life living, and writing, in Italy. In a brief paragraph on the death of Chekhov, he includes a detail I don't remember having come across before. Herling says that in June 1904, just after Chekhov and Knipper arrived in Badenweiler, Chekhov insisted they change hotels because he wanted a room with a balcony. So the couple found another hotel. Nobody ever mentions the balcony. Or that Chekhov spent many of his last hours sitting out there, watching people go in and out of the post office across the street. Imagine him studying each face, what he could see of them from up there, every gesture.

» 93 «

I'VE GOT THE LANGUAGE RIGHT HERE. *I INTENTIONALLY and with full knowledge have made no provision under the terms of this testament for the following:* _____ *and* _____. *The omission of provision is occasioned not by a lack of love.*

I remember sitting in the hospital room. Together we watched a show about primates. The sound was turned down. Earlier, I'd brought him a chocolate milkshake from McDonald's. McDonald's milkshakes were the only thing he'd eat. And then that distant burbling. You know it? The sound you make when you're out of milkshake but you're still searching with your straw for a little more. I thought about the doctor, that glib motherfucker, who told him he'd dance again. My father who never danced. My father whose once strong legs were twigs I could have broken with my fingers.

In the dark, on the TV, those baboons grunted in the trees, their chests rising and falling.

When he'd call I'd never answer. This went on for decades. He'd call multiple times a day and I wouldn't pick up. Before cell phones I could recognize his ring. A certain abruptness that would crack open a still moment.

I do like to talk about it, how he snipped, snipped, snipped me and my brother right out, out, out. People I tell look at me like somebody died. Someone did die. How many times can I make this joke? Words are like ashes. Even in my mind he scatters. The omission of provision. It's not about the money, Rabbi. We kissed when we met, kissed when we parted.

» 94 «

I PICKED IT UP AT THE DUMP. *THE JOURNALS OF JOHN Cheever.* There's a shed where every Saturday people leave grocery bags of books, cardboard boxes of books. Sometimes, people leave the books and take the cardboard box back home. The journals stretch back thirty years, 395 pages of collected despair. The entries lack the comic radiance of his stories. Cheever writes about his drinking. The man swam through decades of alcohol. "Sitting in a chair on the stones before the house drinking Scotch and reading Aeschylus." "I will go to the dentist in a half an hour, and I would like a drink." "We run out of liquor as I had planned, at noon." There are many passages about his long marriage and what he calls his homosexual anxieties. At one point a man—M— is late to meet him and Cheever ponders the difference between waiting for a woman ("a destiny") and waiting for a man ("quite painful"). That's (unintentional) comedy. He writes about his kids, his work. He says that "The Enormous Radio" is overwritten and that "Goodbye My Brother" is "too small." He walks the dog. He has lunch with other writers. Philip Roth complains that his ex-wife won't give him back his ice skates.

In 1961:

I pray that our life in the new house will be peaceful and full. I pray to be absolved of my foolishness and to be returned to the liveliness, the acuteness of feeling, that seems to be my best approach to things.

In 1976, a single line stopped me cold:

So tomorrow I go to Boston to bury my brother.

In the final entry, June 1982, Cheever writes that he's only just made it up to his third-floor study, to his typewriter. He wonders what's happened to the character, the discipline, that's brought him up here day after day after day. Then he jolts, without transition, into these lines:

I think of an early dusk the day before yesterday. My wife is in the garden planting something. "I want to get this in before dark," she will have said. A light rain, a drizzle, is falling.

I'm struck by the shifting tenses. Cheever recounts a moment from the past, as we often do, in the present. In this case, it's the very recent past, the day before yesterday. The third sentence changes everything. What tense is *she will have said*? Future conditional? Is this a thing? Whatever it is, it feels too deliberate to be the mistake of a terminally exhausted man. I wonder if Cheever started to tell himself about a particular dusk, the day before yesterday—his wife, Mary, is in the garden planting something—but this one dusk began to morph, before he reached the end of the sentence, into many dusks stretching across years. It's as if time has already collapsed and, at the same time, extends, reaches. Not only what Mary said, it's what she will have said. The day before yesterday and forever.

I want to get this in before dark.

AGAIN SHE STANDS BY THE BROOK THAT RUNS BY THE house with her hands in the pockets of her coat. The distance between myself standing at the kitchen window and watching and her out in the trees. She'll allow herself to be watched so long as I make no attempt to close the distance.

I'M READING ON THE PORCH OF A RENTED HOUSE IN THE north end of Burlington. My mother is upstairs in a small bedroom, in a narrow bed, trying to sleep. Now she sleeps late. She never used to. Grief's tiring.

It's after ten in June. The Air National Guard is flying training missions over Lake Champlain. These sleek black planes, their sonic boomings.

The house is across the street from a cemetery. Mismatched stones crowd the hillside. *Pike, Dumas, Kane, McAuliffe, Dattilo, Greenough.* Yesterday, wandering around up there, I came across blankets and a camping mattress unfurled at the foot of a grave. A sweatshirt hung off a branch of a nearby tree.

I'm three quarters of the way through Penelope Fitzgerald's *The Beginning of Spring,* past the point where the swath of pages I've read is thicker than what's left. And to finish any Fitzgerald novel is to become immediately bereft that you can no longer read it for the first time. I'm putting that off. I've started *The Beginning of Spring* again.

A family of British expatriates in Moscow before the revolution. In the opening sentence we learn that Frank's wife, Nina, has left him. At first, she took the children with her on a train heading west but changed her mind. During a stopover, Nina sent the kids back to Moscow, back to Frank, and continued on her way. In chapter 2, Frank arrives at the station to retrieve them. Fitzgerald describes the people Frank sees waiting around:

> Lost souls who haunt stations and hospitals in the hope of acquiring some purpose of their own in the presence of so much urgent business, other people's partings, reunions, sickness and death.

I'm thinking about other people's partings when the front door slaps open and my mother, fully dressed and wearing sunglasses and a baseball hat, charges past me, off the porch and out to the sidewalk, shouting at the sky, at all that deafening noise, at all that urgent business, *What the hell's happening?*

Night

Nothing could halt this process, as it gradually became impossible to distinguish leaf from branch, water from rock, even the house from the hillslope behind it.

—EVA FIGES, *Light*

97

IN ALLEN GROSSMAN'S TITLE POEM "THE WOMAN ON the Bridge over the Chicago River" everything weeps. Stars are falling tears. The moon is a sea of tears. The wind weeps. Cormorants and roses weep. Streams and bones, gnats and moths—all are weeping. Eternity and Time itself weep. Being and Nothing, too. Oceans. The sad family next door weeps. Even the love that generates life, the muffled noises of creation, his parents having sex in the next room . . . A boy looks up at the ceiling:

> As the grieving sound of his own begetting
> Keeps on . . .

And a woman in a blue coat weeps into the Chicago River.

If you think of the Chicago River, and why shouldn't you, if you see it glooming down there beneath our streets—they stain it green on St. Patrick's Day and even then it's not festive—you'll know that it's a good place to cry into. There are no banks, only high cement walls that contain the river's wallows. A river subdued, confined, channeled. In order to keep sewage out of Lake Michigan (and sent into the Mississippi instead) they reversed the flow of it in one of the great engineering feats of the last century. Still, the Chicago River is a river. My grandfather's younger brother drowned in it in the mid-'70s. When my grandfather came home after identifying him at the morgue he said to my grandmother, "A man's born in this city, dies in this city. They can't afford to put a sheet over him?"

I bought this copy of *The Woman on the Bridge over the Chicago River* in Iowa City, at a store that no longer exists. Not a store really, just the house of a retired professor. He'd put books in a milk crate on his front porch. If you found something you liked, you took it. Stuffed a buck or two under the floor mat where there were always other stray dollars he never collected.

I wonder how the poem came about. Did Grossman, as a boy, the boy once listening to the mournful noises of his parents on the other side of the wall, once pass by on the bridge one night and happen to see a woman out there in the cold and make a note in his mind not to forget her? For decades he held the vision? Of all the weeping in the universe, it will come down to hers?

A small woman wrapped in an old blue coat

There are some people who aren't afraid to weep in public. You see them in restaurants, on buses. The other day, at a Sunoco in Rutland, I watched a woman on the other side of the island sob as she pumped gas.

» 98 «

IN THE BASEMENT OF THE HOUSE THAT CAME TO BE known only later as my father's house was a small door about a quarter of the size of an ordinary door. When I was five or six the door was perfectly proportionate to my own height. I didn't need to duck to walk right through it. The door opened to a narrow passage that led to a small space behind the furnace and the hot water heater. The door must have been built so an adult on their hands and knees could squeeze behind there to make an adjustment or a repair. Then, it was a place only I knew about, and many nights and some days, too, I'd wedge into that alleyway, a kind of tunnel really. Too dark to read; I'd crouch and listen to myself breathe. A few feet away the constant blue flame of the water heater. The house is gone. A neighbor bought it so he could knock it down and have one neighbor fewer. And when they knocked the house down, 105 Hazel Avenue, an address that no longer exists on any map—think of all the lost addresses, all those coordinates of nowhere—and bulldozed the wreckage, somewhere in that flattened pile of metal and brick and lumber was the little door. I was a weird kid. More lonely than weird. I thought I was weirder than I was. I had some of the usual reasons for retreating down there. Nightly kitchen shouting was only one. It was too dark to read. I could have brought a book and a flashlight. I didn't. Now I see that narrow void as a kind of Jewish kid's confessional. It felt good just to squeeze in there, the blue light in the small distance. I'm repeating myself. Always, lately, I'm repeating myself. Again, this hunger to return to places that are gone from the Illinois earth. As if I murmur it enough to myself, I'll be able to go through that door again without ducking.

» **99** «

Among the last pieces Virginia Woolf is known to have worked on was a four-page story called "The Search-light." There are multiple drafts of the story, the earliest known dated 1929; the latest, 1941. Over the years, she gave it different titles, among them: "What the Telescope Discovered," "A Scene from the Past," as well as "Inaccurate Memories" and "Incongruous."

In January 1939, two years before her death, she noted in her diary, "I wrote the old Henry Taylor telescope story that's been humming in my mind these ten years."

Only the teller and the audience seem to change, who tells the story to whom. From the first draft to the last, the core—a boy and his telescope—remains a constant. A boy lives in isolation on a farm. His family was once affluent and powerful but they've since come down in the world. His parents sit in silence. Nobody ever visits. He spends hours up in an old tower looking through his telescope, scanning the sky. One day the boy lowers the lens and sweeps across the moors. He sees the trees, some birds, a stem of smoke rising from the chimney of a house. He lowers the telescope farther. It's then that the boy spies a young woman emerging from a house. He watches her as she feeds some pigeons. In the last known version, the rotating beam of a wartime searchlight as it scans across London reminds a woman, a Mrs. Ivemey,

275

who's at the theater with some friends, of the story of her grandfather and grandmother. At the play's intermission, she tells the friends about the boy, the telescope, the girl feeding the pigeons.

> And then . . . look . . . A man . . . A man! He came round the corner. He seized her in his arms! They kissed . . . they kissed!

The boy tosses away the telescope, scrambles down the steps of the tower, and begins a mad sprint across the moors— miles he sprints—until, dusty and sweating, he reaches the girl with the pigeons, his future wife.

Someone in her party asks: But what about the other man, the one she kissed?

"Oh, that man," Mrs. Ivemey says, as if to say what does he have to do with anything. "He, I suppose, vanished."

Whatever Woolf called it, the story obviously meant something to her. Why else would she have returned to it again and again? So simple, even obvious. Look at the stars all you want. What you need is down here on the ground. I wonder if she struggled with the story so long because she was searching for a way to believe in it.

A FRIEND OF MINE ONCE WITNESSED A MAN BEING
stomped to death on the sidewalk. This was in San Francisco
in the early 2000s. It was after three in the morning. My friend
called 911. He told the dispatcher that if somebody didn't come
now, right now to the corner of Twenty-Fifth and Hampshire,
they were going to kill this guy. Had it been a different address maybe the cops would have come sooner. Maybe not.
My friend stood by the window. He said that at first the guy on
the sidewalk was screaming. That's what woke him up. But he
said then the screaming gave way to a sound more like yelping.
He said the three guys doing the stomping weren't saying anything at all. They were methodical. This was something they
were doing with their feet. After maybe four, five minutes, the
yelping stopped and there weren't any sounds at all. The three
men seemed to float away, east on Twenty-Fourth, toward Bry-
ant Street, soundless, as if they never existed. My friend said
that when he looked out into the dark at the heap he could
barely make out, he put his hand to his mouth as if to quiet his
own breathing. By then the cops and the paramedics—
   We were at Charlie's, at Precita and Folsom. Charlie's is a
place where you can talk. My friend was telling me this in a
whisper. There was nobody else in the café. It was late morning. Charlie was outside messing around with somebody's
dog. There's a laundromat next door and people tie up their

dogs at the parking meter. Charlie likes to go out there and give them some attention. My friend said it was not so much his cowardice that bothered him as the fact that he'd put his hand over his mouth.

"You know what I mean? Like if I couldn't hear myself, I wasn't there?"

"What were you going to do? Run out there and stop three guys? They'd have beaten the living shit out of you, too. What good would that have done?"

"I'm talking about me standing there," my friend said, "and how my own panting was the problem, like it was about my own failure and not this person—"

I started to tell him about an Isaac Babel story, about this former serf who—

"Do you ever stop? Don't you get tired of yourself?"

"—and then, after joining the Red Army, he returns to his old estate. When he gets there he tramples his former landlord to death. For an hour he tramples and tramples."

"That's just not helpful. And this guy wasn't anybody's landlord."

"How do you know? But the answer is yes, god knows I get so tired of myself that—"

He got up to refill his coffee. If you're a regular, Charlie doesn't charge for refills. Otherwise, it's a buck. My friend sat back down with his coffee.

He said, "That yelping. Like there's got to be sounds inside us we have no idea we carry around. You know? Don't say anything, not a fucking thing."

He stood up, drank a final swig of coffee as if he was about to leave. He sat back down.

» 101 «

THE DEAD SHOULDN'T RETURN. IT'S THE LAST MIRACLE anybody truly wants. Uncle Lazar, a fervent Zionist, immigrates to Palestine from Poland in the '30s, before the establishment of the state of Israel. His childhood sweetheart follows three years later. Love's rekindled. Rachel gets pregnant, and Rachel and Lazar marry and move into a small shack on the edge of the desert. Soon enough there are two children. Though he still believes in the cause, Lazar's commitment to the creation of his own nation evolves into a loyalty to an all-encompassing brotherhood. He resolves to join an international brigade and help defend the Republican government in Spain. Rachel implores him not to leave. The two say hardly a word to each other on the day Uncle Lazar departs for Europe. A few letters follow; then, months later, unofficial word that Uncle Lazar's been killed in action. A few months after that, a letter from Lazar himself, but the date stamp is blurry. It's impossible to tell when the letter was mailed. Another year of rumors. Lazar's dead. Lazar's not dead. And still, no sign of him.

Rachel waits another three years before she remarries.

Meanwhile, Uncle Lazar is in Siberia, having been arrested on charges of being a foreign infiltrator. He's held eighteen years before he's, inexplicably, released.

This is all a fairly marginal episode in Yaakov Shabtai's

Past Continuous. The story of Rachel and Lazar takes up about four and a half pages of the nearly four hundred in the novel.

Needless to say, upon his return to Israel after nearly two decades, Lazar goes to see Rachel and his children.

Hard to explain why this book has been such a relief to me. Maybe it's because of Shabtai's stubborn, at times infuriating, insistence on the past and present being a single entity. How the notion that the past can be separated from the present, as if by some impenetrable wall, is not only false, it's blasphemous to existence. In the novel, the present is the past and the past is the present and the two, often, exist simultaneously in the same sentence, separated only by the inconsequential twip of a comma. What's happened has happened and yet, always, it will keep happening.

In Tel Aviv, Uncle Lazar, who's dead, weeps in the night rain. He's just come from Rachel's house.

The reunion is hardly a scene. Uncle Lazar stands on one side of a table; Rachel and the two grown children on the other. A few words are exchanged, and that's it. It's over. This moment is not the hinge of this novel. In other books it might be. It's only, as I say, one moment among thousands of moments, which is the point, or would be the point if this book was the sort of book to make a point, which thank god it isn't. There's more in it than any reader could possibly keep track of—marriages, children, nieces, nephews, cousins, divorces, affairs, sorrows, rapture, suicide, funerals, war, epic political arguments, sex, health trouble, petty grievances.

How much of our lives are spent nursing petty grievances? In the original Hebrew the novel unfurls over the course of a single paragraph like a scroll.

> She did not shake his hand or invite him to sit down or ask him how he was, and the truth is that the moment she saw him standing in the doorway she wanted to ask him why he had come and tell him to leave, but something of his emotion had infected her, in addition to which she had to contend with her own curiosity, and so she held her tongue, but she felt no sympathy for him.

You might call Uncle Lazar a minor character. Those times he does appear, he's only on stage for a few pages at a time. He comes and he goes like the ghost he's become. I've got a friend who once said minor characters don't know they're minor. It's a quote I've always loved, as it speaks as much to life as it does to fiction, but I wonder if, in this case, Uncle Lazar does know he's minor as he stands across the table from Rachel and the children. Uncle Lazar reaches for his daughter but she backs away. He reaches and he reaches. And maybe this is how it goes. Minor characters don't know they're minor, until they do. And doesn't this, at some point, include us all?

THIS WOULD HAVE BEEN IN THE EARLY '80S. SOMETHING had gone wrong with the chemicals in the water in the high school swimming pool. Overnight, they'd drained it. She'd come in the early mornings to practice. She had her own key to the pool. It was a different time. Everybody had keys to everything. A custodian put up a sign but she missed it.

Debbie Nadler. I never knew her. At least I never spoke to her. She was five or six years older. I knew her brother, Donny. He was in the grade above me. He used to push me around. Donny Nadler was one of those guys who liked to see if you'd take the bait, shout *hey putz* to see if you'd look. I always looked, every single time, which bored him. The Nadlers lived up the street in a house of comings and goings. Debbie had tons of friends. Cars would stop and dump out so many high school kids you wondered how they'd all fit. Laughter, slamming doors, shouts. More cars would come, disgorge more laughter. I'd be riding by on my bike, pretending not to check it all out. They were like a human ant colony. And Debbie, the queen, lying on her back on her front lawn smoking a cigarette, as if all the commotion had nothing to do with her. She looked like I remember girls of that time, long, long hair parted in front like curtains.

Our house was so closed up, locked up. My father

double-locked the doors in the suburbs. Minute you walked in the house, he'd bolt the door—

The lit end of Debbie Nadler's cigarette like a third eye lurking above her head on some gone afternoon. For years after, her name was evoked as a warning. *Look before you jump, remember Debbie Nadler . . .*

My grandmother Sally used to say, What hurts you hurts you. The same might be said of what haunts you.

Those early mornings, how cold it must have been climbing those three or four steps up to the low diving board. In her head, music? Something poppy? "Afternoon Delight"? I read once that music, at its ancient root, is always a response to grief. Even in a song as dumb as "Afternoon Delight" it's there, buried.

As she'd been doing for months as part of her training regimen, still a little groggy, she walked quickly across to the edge of the low dive, a leap and a practiced, easy arc, just warming up, the water would wake her. That expected jolt of cold shock. Was there a point in her descent when she felt on her skin that something was different?

» 103 «

On April 11, 1987, Primo Levi, according to the cor-
oner's report, hurled himself from the landing at the top of
four flights of stairs. There are those, including his widow
and one of his closest friends, who believed that it must have
been a freak accident caused by a medication that brought on
a kind of vertigo. They argued that as a professional chemist
Levi would have known countless other ways to take his life,
ways that wouldn't risk the possibility of becoming maimed
but surviving.

The only certainty we have are his sentences. They remain
intact, whole. No, I won't read Levi backward from April 1987
any more than I'd read Woolf or Celan or anybody else who
took their own life backward. They didn't create from the
grave. Did somebody suggest they did? It's December 2021,
snowless. I've started an argument with myself.

I return to *The Periodic Table*. I read this unclassifiable
book out of order, like I might read the Bible, if I read the
Bible. In "Gold," Levi describes, after his arrest in the mountains, meeting and talking with another prisoner. This was
while Levi was still being held by the somewhat hapless Italian Fascists, before being handed over to the SS.

It was a freezing night, and the guard allowed the two
prisoners a few minutes of heat in the boiler room. This other
prisoner wasn't a Partisan; he'd been arrested for smuggling

contraband, but he lets Levi know that he's sympathetic to the cause and the two begin to talk. It's then that the smuggler tells Levi a fantastic story. He says that there's a stretch of river that's become a birthright in his family. Gold, the smuggler tells Levi, runs through it. He also says if their situations were reversed, if Levi was merely a common prisoner who was going to be released soon, and he, the smuggler, in Levi's shoes, he'd tell him where this stretch of river lies. Levi writes that at that moment he felt wounded, that as a Partisan and a Jew he knew damn well where he stood. Why rub it in? A moment of almost everyday social awkwardness follows as the two stand by the boiler on a freezing night in an Italian prison, with the guard slumped, dozing by the door, a tommy gun in his lap. The smuggler, realizing Levi has taken offense, tries to smooth things over by saying, Well, anyway, there isn't really that much gold. He also tells Levi that should he ever get the chance it's best to pan for gold in good weather. Make sure, the smuggler says, the moon is in the last quarter. The two go silent for a while. Levi's grateful for the quiet. He thinks about the uncertain days ahead.

> Of course I would search for gold: not to get rich
> but to try out a new skill, to see again the earth,
> air, and water from which I was separated by a
> gulf that grew larger every day . . .

» 104 «

Last night Katie and I put the kids to bed in one bed and went to bed ourselves. We're at her mother's place, where there are two extra beds for guests. At about three in the morning, Roscoe came and joined us in our bed. Because he kept kicking me in the head I went to sleep alongside Phoebe in the other bed, but because at that point I couldn't sleep I turned on the flashlight that comes with the phone and started to read. The light bothered Phoebe so she went and joined Katie and Rossy. As that bed was so crowded, Katie got up and joined me. She said, If I don't get some sleep I'll murder somebody.

105

In this little park, at the picnic table, talking to myself. It's a peaceful garden between Vermont Salvage and the old bank building. Except there are signs: Private Property, Trespassers Will Be Prosecuted, This Area Under Video Surveillance. Yet the place is so inviting. I come here a lot, risking the wrath of whoever puts up the signs.

Now, having shoved another novel away from me across the picnic table, I'm staring at the back of the old bank building. There are places where you can see the windows have been bricked in, where the brick is a newer, brighter red. Like parodies of windows. At the same time isn't there something achingly intimate about the outline of where a window used to be?

The person who served me coffee, most days, for a couple of years. His name was Ezra. He committed suicide last month. During the pandemic (I write as if it were over) he once refused my dollar tip because, he said, he was doing all right on unemployment. He said he only came in as a volunteer. As I turned to walk away, he added, "Also, I like having a place to come to." He had a red beard and always wore a red bandana. He was twenty-five. There was a gentleness about him. Ezra took the time to look at you. We forget how difficult this is and how uncommon. Always, at first, he'd look at you before he spoke. Someone, a family member or a friend, wrote a tender obituary that was printed in the *Valley News*, and a fellow employee taped his picture up on the door of the café in tribute. It remained there for weeks until the manager decided it was time to take it down.

106

HE REMEMBERS OVERHEARING A COUPLE THROUGH THE walls of a motel room in 1975. They weren't fighting or having crazy loud sex. They were consoling each other. They were consoling each other because they'd both lived out their lives and it was useless to argue about the things they used to argue about, like money or a daughter staying out all night. They also now understood what they should have known all along. Neither of them was ever going to change. A poet in the next room was listening. He may have been drunk; he often was, but I don't think so, not that night. Years later, Larry Levis would remember and write about those two. About how there was relief in the voices he heard through the walls. A few lines later, the poem shifts away from the motel. The couple has split up. Or maybe one of them has died. In any case, Levis imagines one of them, it doesn't seem to matter which one, in a kitchen, checking to see if the water on the stove is boiling. He describes the gray day, the sky as it is reflected in the water in the pot and the way the sun, what little of it there is, illuminates a spiked clematis on the windowsill. The quiet kitchen of a quiet house. A pot on a stove. I have a recurring image of someone alone in an apartment by the highway. There's rain. I'm looking out a window at night, at the blurred red taillights.

» 107 «

We were on the Kennedy, heading north, when my mother said, "Every time I pass the Irving Park exit I think of spending the night in the gas station."

"What?"

"The Blizzard of '78," she said, "even though by then it was January of '79 but we still called it the Blizzard of '78. That winter, it snowed for centuries—"

"I remember."

"I was driving home from teaching, this was when I was at Lane Tech, and I was on the expressway. At a certain point I couldn't see two inches in front of me and anyway the car had stopped moving forward. It was dark but at the same time it was like the whole earth was being smothered to death by a white blanket. My wheels were spinning and spinning. I left the car on the highway, which wasn't even a highway anymore, and trudged through the drifting snow to the Irving Park exit. After a few blocks, I found an open gas station. From a pay phone I called Dad at home and he said, 'Well, what do you want me to do about it?'"

"So you slept in the station?"

"No. I didn't sleep. Nobody slept. There were other people stranded. We stood around drinking coffee until morning. Then I somehow managed to convince a cabdriver to bring me home. A couple of weeks later the Chicago police called and said they'd found the Volkswagen. They'd towed it off the Kennedy and dumped it on a side street. It had been stripped. The tires were gone, the dashboard, everything. They dropped off what was left of it at the house on a flatbed truck."

In 1979, my mother was forty-one.

I call my brother.

"She slept in a gas station?"

"She didn't sleep. She said she was up all night."

"I don't remember that," he says.

"She said Dad wouldn't pick her up."

"That part I believe."

All those hours. I'm sure there would have been talk, stories, laughter. I think of the light, the fierce fluorescent light. Eating candy, potato chips just to pass some time. The grime on the walls so caked it was prehistoric. The snow not falling but flinging itself into, beating, the plate glass. My mother and others in a Union 76 station on Irving Park Road, waiting on the dawn.

My brother calls me back.

"One night she didn't come home," he says. "I don't remember the blizzard. I mean I do but not that they were connected. Only that this one night she was gone, she didn't come home—you were asleep—and I thought she wasn't coming back at all."

Sources

1. Edna O'Brien, *House of Splendid Isolation* (New York: Plume, 1995).

2. James Salter, *Dusk* (San Francisco: North Point Press, 1988).

5. Amy Clampitt, *Westward* (New York: Knopf, 1990). Anton Chekhov, *The Steppe and Other Stories*, trans. Ronald Wilks (New York: Penguin Classics, 2002).

6. Lawrence Ferlinghetti, *A Coney Island of the Mind* (New York: New Directions, 1959).

7. Jean Rhys, *The Left Bank and Other Stories* (Freeport, NY: Books for Libraries Press, 1970).

9. Gina Berriault, *The Tea Ceremony: The Uncollected Writings of Gina Berriault* (Berkeley: Counterpoint, 2004).

11. Robert Haas, "My Mother's Nipples," *The Apple Trees at Olema: New and Selected Poems* (New York: Ecco, 2010).

13. Louis-Ferdinand Céline, *Journey to the End of the Night*, trans. Ralph Manheim (New York: New Directions, 1983).

15. William Bronk, "Walt Whitman's Marine Democracy," in *Vectors and Smoothable Curves* (San Francisco: North Point Press, 1985).

16. Isaac Bashevis Singer, *Short Friday* (New York: Penguin, 1984).

18. Eva Figes, *Light* (New York: Pantheon, 1983).

19. Richard Wright, *Haiku: The Last Poems of an American Icon* (New York: Arcade, 2012).

21. Robert Hayden, *Selected Poems* (New York: October House, 1966).

23. Franz Kafka, "The Truth About Sancho Panza," in *Konundrum: Selected Prose of Franz Kafka* (Brooklyn: Archipelago, 2016).

25. Wright Morris, *Plains Song* (Lincoln: University of Nebraska Press, 2000).

26. Donald Justice, *Night Light* (Middletown, CT: Wesleyan University Press, 1967). William Tecumseh Sherman, *Memoirs* (Penguin: New York, 2000).

27. Maeve Brennan, *The Springs of Affection* (Berkeley: Counterpoint, 2009).

29. Nathaniel Hawthorne, *The Scarlet Letter* (New York: Penguin Classics, 2015).

31. James Wright, *Above the River* (New York: Farrar, Straus and Giroux, 1992).

33. Marilynne Robinson, *Home* (New York: Farrar, Straus and Giroux, 2008).

35. Maeve Brennan, *The Long-Winded Lady* (Berkeley: Counterpoint, 2015). Angela Bourke, *Maeve Brennan: Homesick at The New Yorker* (Berkeley: Counterpoint, 2016).

36. Hayden, *Selected Poems.*

37. Ellen Wilbur, *Wind and Birds and Human Voices* (Winston-Salem: Stuart Wright Publishers, 1984).

38. Pier Paolo Pasolini, *Roman Poems* (San Francisco: City Lights, 1986).

40. Arthur Miller, *Death of a Salesman* (New York: Penguin Classics, 1988).

42. Isaac Babel, *Collected Stories*, trans. David McDuff (New York: Penguin Classics, 1995).

44. Rita Dove, *Thomas and Beulah* (Pittsburgh: Carnegie Mellon Poetry Series, 1986).

45. Yoel Hoffman, *Katschen & The Book of Joseph*, trans. David Kriss, Alan Treister, and Eddie Levenston (New York: New Directions, 1988); *Moods*, trans. Peter Cole (New York: New Directions, 2015).

46. Bette Howland, *W-3* (New York: A Public Space Books, 2021).

48. Gordon Bowker, *James Joyce: A New Biography* (New York: Farrar, Straus and Giroux, 2012).

49. James Joyce, *Ulysses* (New York: Vintage, 1990).

51. James Alan McPherson, *Hue and Cry* (Boston: Little, Brown and Co., 1969).

52. Robert Lowell, *Life Studies and For the Union Dead* (New York: Farrar, Straus and Giroux, 1967).

53. Terrance Hayes, *To Float in the Space Between: A Life and Work in Conversation with the Life and Work of Etheridge Knight* (Seattle: Wave Books, 2018). Etheridge Knight, *The Essential Etheridge Knight* (Pittsburgh: University of Pittsburgh Press, 1986).

54. Ella Leffland, *Mrs. Munck* (Boston: Houghton Mifflin, 1970).

57. Tomas Tranströmer, *The Great Enigma: New Collected Poems* (New York: New Directions, 2006).

58. Lorraine Hansberry, *The Sign in Sidney Brustein's Window* (New York: Random House Plays, 1965).

60. Gary Lutz, *The Complete Gary Lutz* (Brooklyn: Tyrant Books, 2019).

61. Stacy Doris, *Knot* (Athens: University of Georgia Press, 2006); *Conference* (Bedford, MA: Poets and Poets Press, 2000).

62. Mario Vargas Llosa, *The Oxford Book of Latin American Essays*, ed. Ilan Stavans (Oxford, UK: Oxford University Press, 1997).

64. Héctor Viel Temperley, *The Last Books of Héctor Viel Temperley* (Key West: Sand Paper Press, 2011).

65. Bernard Malamud, *Idiots First* (New York: Farrar, Straus and Giroux, 1963).

66. Kate Zambreno, *Book of Mutter* (Cambridge, MA: Semiotext(e), 2017).

68. Juan Rulfo, *Pedro Páramo* (New York: Grove Press, 1994).

69. Shirley Hazzard, *The Evening of the Holiday* (New York: Picador, 1990).

71. Pablo Neruda, "Epithalamium," in *The Captain's Verses* (New York: New Directions, 2009).

73. Anton Chekhov, *About Love and Other Stories* (Oxford, UK: Oxford University Press, 2008).

75. Paul Celan, letter to Eric Celan, December 15, 1968, trans. Pierre Joris, in *Paul Celan: Selections,* ed. Pierre Joris (Berkeley: University of California Press, 2005); *Glottal Stop*, trans. Nikolai Popov and Heather McHugh (Hanover, NH: University Press of New England, 2000). John Felstiner, *Paul Celan: Poet, Survivor, Jew* (New Haven: Yale University Press, 2001).

77. Reiner Stach, *Kafka: The Years of Insight*, trans. Shelley Frisch (Princeton: Princeton University Press, 2013). *Konundrum: Selected Prose of Franz Kafka*, trans. Peter Wortsman (Brooklyn: Archipelago, 2016).

78. Elizabeth Tallent, *Honey* (New York: Vintage, 1994).

79. Bernadette Mayer, *Midwinter Day* (New York: New Directions, 1999).

81. Marilynne Robinson, *Home* (New York: Farrar, Straus and Giroux, 2008); *Jack* (New York: Farrar, Straus and Giroux, 2020).

85. Hermione Lee, *Virginia Woolf* (New York: Knopf, 1997).

87. Primo Levi, *The Periodic Table* (New York: Shocken Books, 1986); *The Drowned and the Saved* (New York: Vintage, 1989).

88. Levi, *The Periodic Table.*

89. Andre Dubus, *Dancing After Hours* (New York: Knopf, 1996).

90. William Faulkner, *As I Lay Dying* (New York: Vintage, 1991).

91. Yusef Komunyakaa, *The Chameleon Couch* (New York: Farrar, Straus and Giroux, 2011).

92. Gustaw Herling, *Volcano and Miracle: A Selection from The Journal Written at Night* (New York: Penguin, 1997.)

94. John Cheever, *The Journals of John Cheever* (New York: Knopf, 1991).

96. Penelope Fitzgerald, *The Beginning of Spring* (New York: Holt, 1989).

97. Allen Grossman, *The Woman on the Bridge over the Chicago River* (New York: New Directions, 1979).

99. Virginia Woolf, *The Complete Shorter Fiction of Virginia Woolf*, ed. Susan Dick (New York: Mariner, 1989). Lee, *Virginia Woolf.*

101. Yaakov Shabtai, *Past Continuous* (New York: Schocken, 1989).

103. Levi, *The Periodic Table.*

106. Larry Levis, *The Selected Levis* (Pittsburgh: University of Pittsburgh Press, 2003).

Acknowledgments

Thank you to Daniel Gumbiner of *The Believer*, where a number of these essays first appeared in a different form as part of an irregular column called "Notes in the Margin." A version of section 25 appeared in *The New York Times* as "In Praise of Wright Morris." Thanks as well to the editors of *Harper's*, *The Paris Review*, *Conjunctions*, *Guernica*, *Gulf Coast*, and *Tin House*, where other essays appeared, likewise in a different form.

As always, my thanks to Ellen Levine for her steadfast faith. The world lost a dedicated physician with the passing of Dr. Ivan Strausz in 2019, and I lost an astute and generous reader. You are greatly missed, Ivan.

I've had the luck to work with the legendary Pat Strachan on six books. Thank you, Pat, for your unparalleled eye and for putting up with me all these years.

Many thanks to the patient and exacting Wah-Ming Chang, as well as to Olenka Burgess, tracy danes, Elana Rosenthal, Dana Li, Selihah White, Rachel Fershleiser, Megan Fishmann, Megha Majumdar, and Alicia Kroell at Catapult, and to copy editor John McGhee, and to Martha Wydysh and Audrey Crooks at Trident Media.

And speaking of putting up with me and then some:

Vievee Francis, Bill Craig, Sally Brady, John Griesemer, Nick Regiacorte, Eric Orner, Rob Preskill, Melissa Kirsch, Alex Gordon, Mathew Goshko, Angie Del Campo, and Ricardo Siri. I'm also grateful to MacDowell and Dartmouth College for the gift of time.